The Comic Book ENCYCLOPEDIA of Pro Wrestling

WRITTEN BY JOHN CROWTHER

EDITED BY KEVIN LaPORTE

VOLUME ONE

SQUARED CIRCLE

INVERSE
inversepress.com
facebook.com/inversepress
instagram: inverse_press
@inversepress
SQUARED CIRCLE
wrestlingcomics.com
facebook.com/squaredcirclecomics
instagram: squared_circle_comics
@prowrestlingbio

The Comic Book Encyclopedia of Pro Wrestling

Written by JOHN CROWTHER
Edited by KEVIN LaPORTE

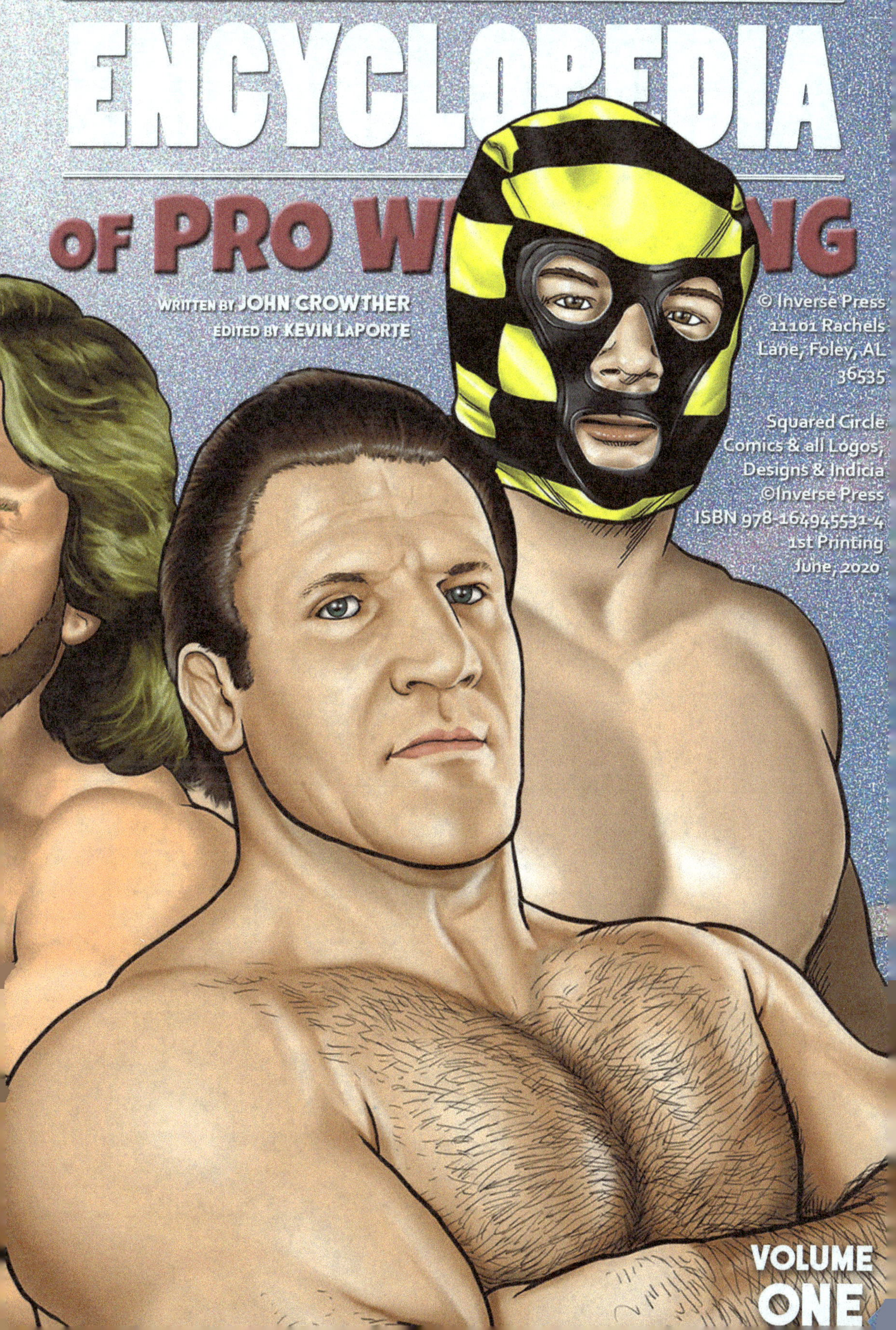

11101 Rachels Lane, Foley, AL 36535

ISBN 978-164945531-4
1st Printing
June, 2020

VOLUME ONE

THE COMIC BOOK ENCYCLOPEDIA OF PRO WRESTLING

TABLE OF CONTENTS

WRESTLER BIOGRAPHIES*
WRITTEN BY JOHN CROWTHER

*ARTISTS & OTHER CONTRIBUTORS ARE CREDITED INDIVIDUALLY WITH EACH STORY.

ENCYCLOPEDIA ENTRIES
WRITTEN BY KEVIN LAPORTE

Bruno Sammartino

The Developmental Years

Born:	October 6, 1935 Pizzoferrato, Italy
Died:	April 18, 2018 Pittsburgh, PA
Spouse:	Carol (m. 1959)
Height:	5' 10"
Weight:	265 lbs
Career:	1959-87

Art by Nathan Smith

When his father, Alfonso, left Italy for the United States during his infancy, Bruno Sammartino was raised in the small mountain village of Pizzoferrato by his mother, Emilia, along with siblings Paul and Mary.

In 1944, Bruno's family was caught in the final battles of World War II, as Pizzoferrato was invaded by German soldiers, forcing them to flee to nearby Valla Rocca.

Dodging heavy shelling, they made it to the mountain camp and hid there for fourteen harrowing months until the end of the War. Unwilling to rebuild their life lost in Pizzoferrato, Emilia planned to take her family to the United States to reunite with Alfonso, but the malnourished Bruno failed his immigration physical, then a requirement for immigration. He was unable to pass the physical for nearly five years, when, in 1950, the Sammartino family finally embarked to America.

They settled in Pittsburgh, where Bruno encountered poverty and bullying in school before meeting friend, Maurice Simon, who introduced him to weight-lifting. Bruno saw quick results and soon joined the Young Men's Hebrew Association gym, where his initial interest in wrestling was sparked. A supportive high school teacher connected him with Rex Peery, wrestling coach at the University of Pittsburgh, and he began training with the college team. Concerned about academics, he turned down a wrestling scholarship and turned, instead, to power lifting competitions, where he found his first great successes, years before making his mark in the squared circle.

writer	**John E. Crowther** @crowman1971
artist	**Rich Perotta** @RichPerottaArt
colorist	**Vito Potenza** @PiwiTFP
editor/ designer	**Kevin LaPorte** @kevinlaporte

PIZZOFERRATO, ITALY. 1944.
I WAS BORN ON OCTOBER 6, 1935, IN THE VILLAGE OF PIZZOFERRATO, LOCATED IN THE APENNINE MOUNTAINS OF CENTRAL ITALY. "THE OLD COUNTRY".
IN PIZZOFERRATO, WE WERE RAISED BY OUR MOTHER, EMILIA.
OUR FATHER, ALFONSO, LEFT FOR THE UNITED STATES WHEN I WAS SIX MONTHS OLD, WITH DREAMS OF SECURING WORK, SO HE COULD PROVIDE A FUTURE HOME FOR MY MOTHER AND HIS CHILDREN.
VIENI RAGAZZI! GATHER SOME CORN AND POTATOES. HELP YOUR MAMMA!
TAKE THESE TO MAMMA.
MY MOTHER KEPT THE FAMILY TOGETHER WHILE MY FATHER WAS AWAY, RAISING ME, ALONG WITH MY OLDER BROTHER PAUL.
AND MY OLDER SISTER, MARY.
GRAZIE, BRUNO. NOW GET CLEANED UP FOR DINNER.
WE LED A SIMPLE LIFE, ME AND MY FAMILY.

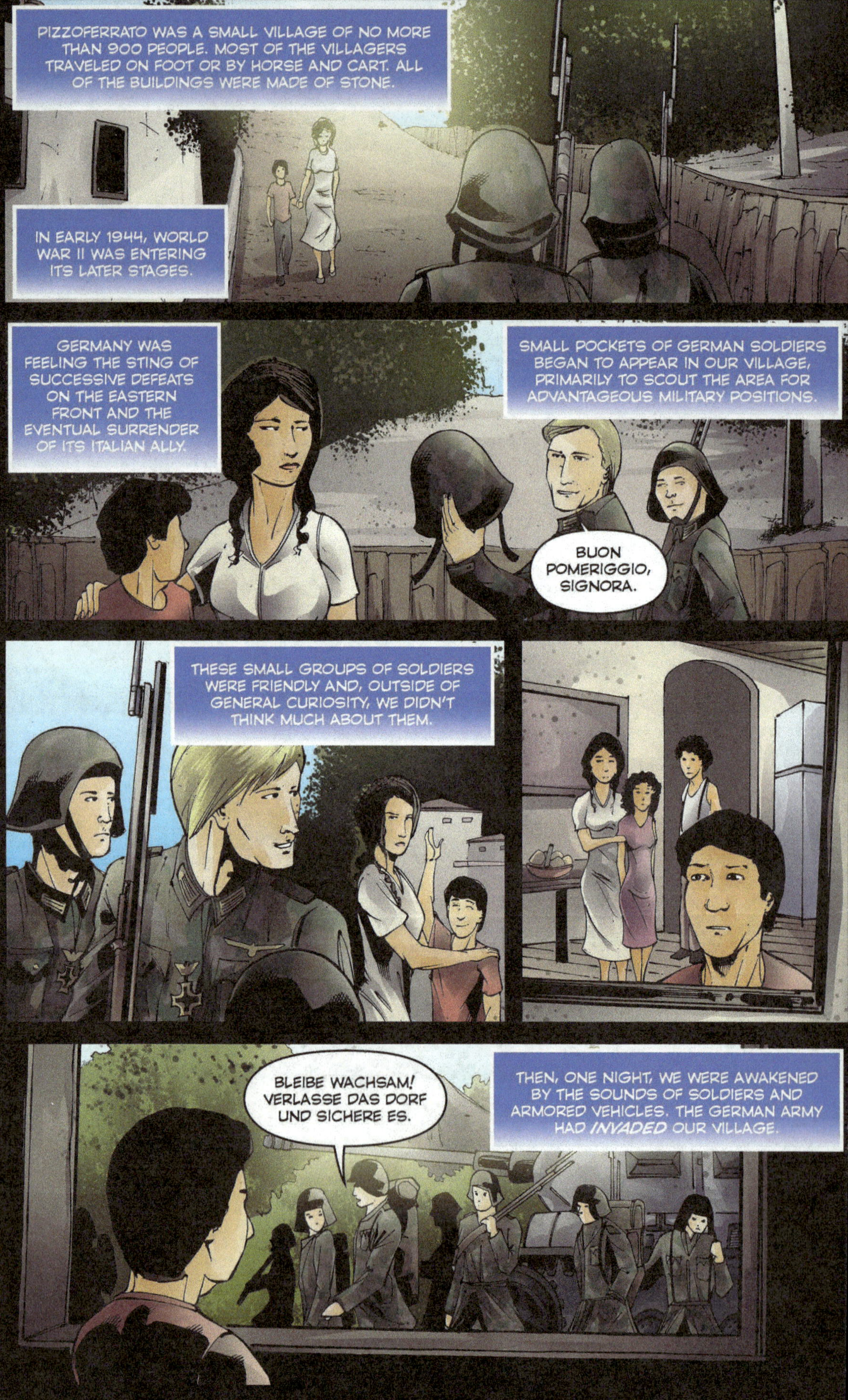

PIZZOFERRATO WAS A SMALL VILLAGE OF NO MORE THAN 900 PEOPLE. MOST OF THE VILLAGERS TRAVELED ON FOOT OR BY HORSE AND CART. ALL OF THE BUILDINGS WERE MADE OF STONE.

IN EARLY 1944, WORLD WAR II WAS ENTERING ITS LATER STAGES.

GERMANY WAS FEELING THE STING OF SUCCESSIVE DEFEATS ON THE EASTERN FRONT AND THE EVENTUAL SURRENDER OF ITS ITALIAN ALLY.

SMALL POCKETS OF GERMAN SOLDIERS BEGAN TO APPEAR IN OUR VILLAGE, PRIMARILY TO SCOUT THE AREA FOR ADVANTAGEOUS MILITARY POSITIONS.

BUON POMERIGGIO, SIGNORA.

THESE SMALL GROUPS OF SOLDIERS WERE FRIENDLY AND, OUTSIDE OF GENERAL CURIOSITY, WE DIDN'T THINK MUCH ABOUT THEM.

KNOCK KNOCK
APRI LA PORTA. IT IS YOUR UNCLE CAMILLO.
MY UNCLE CAMILLO WAS A *PARTISAN*, ASSISTING THE ALLIES IN THEIR MOVEMENT THROUGH THE MOUNTAINS.
LISTEN TO ME, EMILIA. HITLER'S *SS* HAVE ARRIVED. IT IS NO LONGER SAFE TO STAY HERE. GATHER WHAT YOU CAN CARRY AND *LEAVE*.
THESE MEN WERE MUCH DIFFERENT THAN THE SOLDIERS WHO INITIALLY CAME TO THE VILLAGE.
WHERE WILL WE GO?
GO TO ALFONSO'S. HIS FARMHOUSE IS IN THE FIELDS AND FURTHER FROM TOWN. YOU SHOULD BE SAFER THERE.
I REMEMBER BEING *TERRIFIED*, RUNNING THROUGH THE NIGHT WITH NOTHING BUT THE CLOTHES WE WORE, UNTIL WE CAME TO THE FARMHOUSE OF MY UNCLE ALFONSO.

OUR STAY IN THE FARMHOUSE WAS BRIEF. ALLIED FORCES, LED BY THE ENGLISH MILITARY IN THE NEARBY TOWN OF CASTELL, WERE BOMBARDING THE AREA AND TRYING TO DRIVE THE GERMAN FORCES AWAY. MY MOTHER FEARED FOR OUR SAFETY.
BECAUSE THE ALLIES WERE NOT AWARE OF THE EXACT GERMAN POSITIONS, THEIR BOMBING WAS ERRATIC, AND WE OFTEN FOUND OURSELVES IN THE LINE OF FIRE.
IT'S NOT SAFE HERE. IF ONE OF THOSE BOMBS HITS THIS HOUSE, WE'LL ALL BE KILLED.
IT IS SAFER TO STAY IN THE...
NO! I HAVE BEEN TOLD OF A SAFE PLACE ON VALLA ROCCA. MANY PEOPLE FROM THE VILLAGE ARE THERE NOW.
ABBASTANZA! WE ARE LEAVING FOR VALLA ROCCA. STAY IF YOU LIKE, BUT THE LORD HELPS THOSE WHO HELP THEM-SELVES.

FOR TWO DAYS, WE RAN AND CLIMBED UP THE SLOPES OF VALLA ROCCA.
EVERY SO OFTEN, A BOMB WOULD FALL NEARBY, *SHOWERING US* WITH DIRT AND DEBRIS.
BUT MY MOTHER WAS STOIC IN LEADING US TO THE SAFETY OF THE MOUNTAIN CAMP.

WELCOME TO VALLA ROCCA. VENIRE. VENIRE.
PLEASE, WE NEED A PLACE TO STAY. MY HUSBAND IS IN AMERICA, AND IT IS JUST ME AND THE CHILDREN.
YOU WILL BE *SAFE* HERE. COME WITH ME. YOU AND YOUR CHILDREN CAN STAY IN ONE OF MY SHELTERS.
IT ISN'T MUCH, BUT YOU WILL BE SAFE.
THIS WAS OUR HOME FOR NEARLY FOURTEEN MONTHS. IN THE FALL, NIGHTS WERE COLD AND, WITH NOTHING TO WARM US BUT THE SOLITARY FIRE IN THE MIDDLE OF OUR SHELTER, I PASSED THE TIME BY WATCHING THE SMOKE RISE THROUGH THE HOLE IN THE SHELTER'S ROOF.
FOOD WAS SCARCE. IT WAS A STRUGGLE TO SURVIVE. OFTENTIMES, MY MOTHER TRAVELED DOWN THE MOUNTAIN AND SNUCK INTO OUT FORMER HOUSE TO STEAL FOOD FROM THE GERMAN SOLDIERS WHO NOW MADE IT THEIR HOME.

OUR CAMP WAS WELL-SITUATED, AND, FOR THE MOST PART, WE WERE ABLE TO AVOID DETECTION FROM THE GERMAN FORCES, ALTHOUGH THEY ACTIVELY SEARCHED FOR THE "MISSING" VILLAGERS WHO WERE ASSISTING THE ALLIES.
HOWEVER, ON ONE OCCASION, WHILE THE MEN OF THE CAMP WERE AWAY IN SEARCH OF PROVISIONS, THE CAMP WAS DISCOVERED BY A PATROL OF THREE GERMAN SS SOLDIERS.
HERAUSKOMMEN. HERAUSKOMMEN! OR WE WILL SHOOT.
THE SOLDIERS LINED US UP AND BEGAN ASSEMBLING THEIR MACHINE GUN IN PREPARATION FOR A MASS EXECUTION.
DON'T BE AFRAID, MY CHILDREN. SOON, WE WILL BE IN HEAVEN.
THANKFULLY, NONE OF US WOULD DIE THAT THAT DAY, FOR A GROUP OF VILLAGE HUNTERS RETURNED TO CAMP AND KILLED THE GERMAN SOLDIERS BEFORE THEY COULD FIRE THEIR WEAPON. HEAVEN WOULD HAVE TO WAIT.

THERE WERE BODIES *EVERYWHERE*. CORPSES OF VILLAGERS, ALONG WITH THOSE OF ENGLISH, GERMAN, AND POLISH SOLDIERS, AND IT FELL UPON THE RETURNING VILLAGERS TO REBUILD, SOMETHING MY MOTHER WAS *NOT* PREPARED TO DO.

AT THE CONCLUSION OF THE WAR, MY MOTHER MADE CONTACT WITH MY FATHER, WHO WAS STILL LIVING IN THE UNITED STATES.

My dearest Emilia,

These have been the longest years of my life, worrying about your safety and the well-being of our beloved children.

I have made arrangements for you to join me in America by transport on the ship, Saturnia, which sails from Naples to the port of New York.

I long for the time when our family can once again be united. Tutto il mio amore.

Tuo marito,

Alfonso Sammartino

NAPLES, ITALY.
1950.
IMMIGRATION QUOTAS, FOLLOWING THE WAR, REQUIRED IMMIGRANTS TO THE UNITED STATES TO PASS A PHYSICAL. DUE TO MALNOURISHMENT FROM MY MONTHS IN EXILE, I *FAILED* MY PHYSICAL IN MY FIRST ATTEMPT IN 1948.
SO, IT WASN'T UNTIL MY HEALTH IMPROVED THAT WE WERE FINALLY CLEARED TO MAKE OUR JOURNEY TO THE UNITED STATES IN 1950.
WE SET SAIL ON A 14-DAY JOURNEY FROM NAPLES TO NEW YORK CITY ON THE ITALIAN CRUISE LINER, *SATURNIA*. IT WAS *NO* LUXURY LINER. IF YOU WEREN'T SLEEPING, YOU WERE *SEASICK*.
WHEN WE ARRIVED IN NEW YORK CITY, MY FATHER WAS A STRANGER TO US. AS WE HADN'T SEEN HIM IN MANY YEARS, WE WERE AT A LOSS AS TO WHO TO LOOK FOR IN THE MASSIVE CROWD.
EMILIA?
BUT MY FATHER *KNEW* HIS FAMILY.
ALFONSO! ALFONSO!

IN NEW YORK CITY, WE BOARDED A TRAIN THAT, FOLLOWING A BRIEF STOP IN PHILADELPHIA, TOOK US TO OUR NEW HOME IN PITTS-BURGH, PENNSYLVANIA.
AS A CHILD IN ITALY, I HEARD THAT IN AMERICA THE STREETS WERE PAVED WITH GOLD. I BELIEVED THAT YOU COULD LITERALLY REACH DOWN AND SCOOP *GOLD* FROM THE STREETS.
THIS WAS *NOT* THE AMERICA I SAW WHEN I ARRIVED IN PITTSBURGH.
1313
SOLD
WHAT I SAW WAS A *FILTHY*, SMOKY CITY FILLED WITH POVERTY, A FAR CRY FROM THE *BEAUTIFUL*, MOUNTAINOUS REGION IN WHICH I WAS RAISED IN CENTRAL ITALY.
AND OUR NEW HOME WAS NO BETTER. I WAS ACCUSTOMED TO A SMALL, BUT SOLIDLY BUILT, HOUSE OF STONE IN PIZZOFERRATO; MY HOME IN PITTSBURGH WAS A POORLY CONSTRUCTED BRICK HOUSE WITH WALLPAPER PEELING FROM THE WALLS.

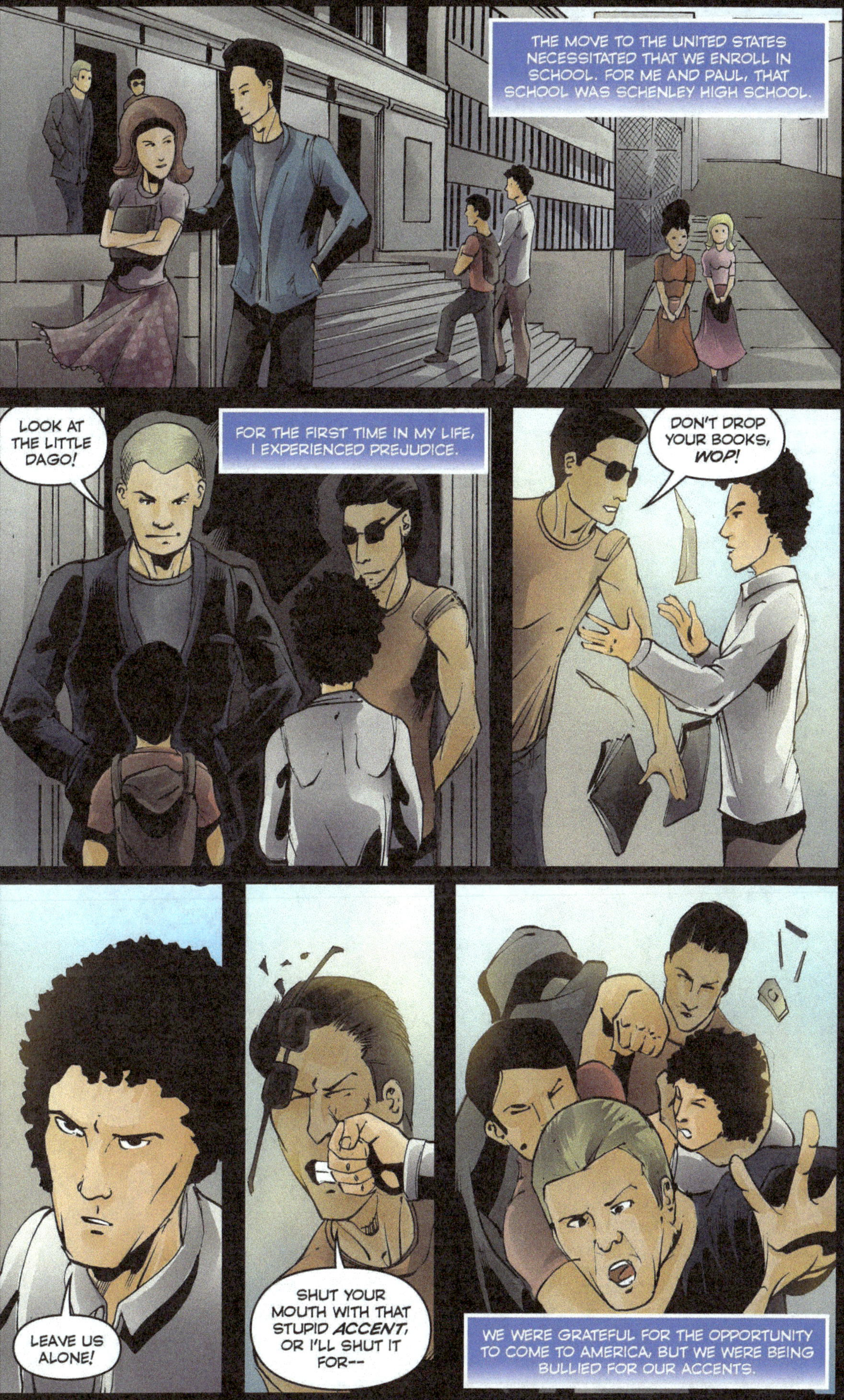

THE MOVE TO THE UNITED STATES NECESSITATED THAT WE ENROLL IN SCHOOL. FOR ME AND PAUL, THAT SCHOOL WAS SCHENLEY HIGH SCHOOL.

YOU GUYS ARE GETTING A *BUM RAP*. YOU SHOULDN'T HAVE TO DEAL WITH THAT.
YEAH, THOSE GUYS ARE *HUGE*.
THAT'S EASY ENOUGH TO *SAY*...
NOT EVERYONE TREATED US BADLY. ONE SUCH PERSON WAS OUR FRIEND, MAURICE SIMON, A YOUNG JEWISH KID WHO NOTICED HOW WE WERE BULLIED.
YOU JUST GOTTA *WORK OUT*. THAT'S ALL. YOU SHOULD COME TO THE YMHA AND WORK OUT WITH ME.
YMHA? WHAT'S THAT?
THE YOUNG MEN'S HEBREW ASSOCIATION. THEY'VE GOT A GYM. $11 TO JOIN.
THANKS, BUT...WE CAN'T AFFORD IT.
PAUL AND I COULDN'T AFFORD THE COST OF THE YMHA BUT, FROM THE MONEY WE WERE ABLE TO SAVE FROM THE PART-TIME CONSTRUCTION JOBS WE BOTH WORKED, WE WERE ABLE TO SCRAPE UP ENOUGH TO PURCHASE A COURSE GUIDE FOR A WEIGHT-TRAINING PROGRAM WE HAD READ ABOUT...
...THE CHARLES ATLAS STRENGTH BUILDING COURSE.

WHEN THE CHARLES ATLAS COURSE BOOK ARRIVED, PAUL AND I IMMEDIATELY TOOK TO THE BASEMENT AND PUT IT TO USE, LEARNING ABOUT "DYNAMIC TENSION", AND DOING PUSH-UPS AND SIT-UPS FOR HOURS. THE RESULTS WERE READILY APPARENT.

I LIKED THE PHYSICAL CHANGES I WAS SEEING FROM THE CHARLES ATLAS PROGRAM, BUT IT HAD ITS LIMITS.
I WANTED TO GET MORE SERIOUS ABOUT BODYBUILDING, SO I APPROACHED MY MOTHER ABOUT JOINING THE YMHA.
OKAY, BRUNO. WHY DON'T YOU AND PAUL SAVE A LITTLE FROM YOUR PAYCHECKS AND USE THAT TO GET THE MEMBERSHIP.
THANK YOU, MAMMA.
WE FOLLOWED OUR MOTHER'S ADVICE, AND, SOON, PAUL AND I BEGAN TRAINING AT THE YMHA. I BECAME *ADDICTED* TO IT. I TRULY BELIEVED THAT BODYBUILDING WAS MY DESTINY.
I ALSO BECAME INTERESTED IN WRESTLING, ENCOURAGING YOUNG MEN FROM MY HIGH SCHOOL GYM CLASS AND FOOTBALL TEAM TO WORK OUT WITH ME ON THE MAT.
I WAS DETERMINED TO *NEVER AGAIN* BE THE SKINNY KID THAT WAS PUSHED AROUND.
SCHENLEY HIGH SCHOOL DID NOT HAVE A WRESTLING TEAM, BUT MY GYM TEACHER AND FOOTBALL COACH, MR. GROSS, SAW MY INTEREST IN WRESTLING AND APPROACHED ME.
YOU'VE GOT TALENT, SON. AND I'D HATE TO SEE IT WASTED.
THANKS, COACH.
I WANT YOU TO CONTACT MY FRIEND AT PITT, *REX PEERY*. HE'S THE WRESTLING COACH OVER THERE. I'VE TOLD HIM ABOUT YOU AND HE'S WILLING TO LET YOU WORK OUT WITH THE TEAM. IT'S A GREAT OPPORTUNITY FOR YOU, BRUNO.

I TOOK THE ADVICE OF MR. GROSS AND, AFTER SCHOOL, I MADE THE WALK UP "CARDIAC HILL" FROM SCHENLEY HIGH SCHOOL TO THE PITT FIELD HOUSE TO TRAIN WITH COACH PEERY AND THE UNIVERSITY OF PITTSBURGH WRESTLING TEAM.
WHEN I FIRST ENTERED THE FIELD HOUSE, I WAS IN *AWE*.
HERE I WAS, A HIGH SCHOOL KID, AND I WOULD BE TRAINING WITH FUTURE OLYMPIANS, AS WELL AS PAN AMERICAN AND NATIONAL AU CHAMPIONS.
IT DIDN'T TAKE LONG BEFORE COACH PEERY HAD ME MIXING IT UP WITH HIS WRESTLERS.
COACH
COACH
WHAT ARE YOU GAWKING AT, SAMMARTINO? ***GET IN THERE!***
"GET IN THERE", I DID. NOT WITH ANY ONE PARTICULAR PITT WRESTLER, BUT WITH ANYONE WHO WAS WILLING TO TAKE ME ON.

MY SENIOR YEAR IN HIGH SCHOOL, I WAS OFFERED A SCHOLARSHIP TO WRESTLE FOR THE UNIVERSITY. IT WAS A YEAR-TO-YEAR DEAL, MEANING I WOULD HAVE TO PROVE MYSELF WITH MY GRADES EACH YEAR TO MAINTAIN THE SCHOLARSHIP.
WHY YOU WASTING YOUR TIME WITH THE SCHOOLING, BRUNO? IT DOES *NOTHING* FOR YOU.
WHAT SHOULD I DO, DAD?
WHAT YOU'RE GOOD AT, BRUNO. CARPENTRY. YOU SHOULD DO CARPENTRY.
I HAD LITTLE CONFIDENCE IN MY ACADEMIC ABILITIES AND TURNED IT DOWN, RELYING ON THE ADVICE OF MY FATHER.
CARPENTRY WAS WHAT I WAS GOOD AT, SO LEARNING THE TRADE WAS WHAT I WOULD DO...
...BUT I ALSO CONTINUED TO TRAIN.

BUT TRAINING WASN'T ENOUGH. I FELT THE URGE TO COMPETE, AND, SOON, I WAS ENTERING AND WINNING POWER LIFTING COMPETITIONS, AT FIRST NOVICE, THEN JUNIOR, SENIOR STATE AND, EVENTUALLY, NATIONAL MEETS.
MY TRAINING PARTNER AT THE TIME WAS A YOUNG MAN NAMED ALEX PHILIN. ALEX WAS ALSO A COMPETITIVE BODYBUILDER, AND HE ENCOURAGED ME TO PURSUE THE SPORT.
ALEX WAS MORE THAN A TRAINING PARTNER. IN THE SUMMER OF 1955, ALEX AND HIS GIRLFRIEND INTRODUCED ME TO THE GIRL WHO WOULD LATER BECOME MY WIFE AND MOTHER OF MY CHILDREN, CAROL.
I COULDN'T BE HAPPIER. I WAS STILL TRAINING, COMPETING, AND DATING THE GIRL OF MY DREAMS.

BUT, IN THE SUMMER OF 1957, I WAS LAID OFF, AND THE UNITED STATES' INVOLVEMENT IN VIETNAM WAS ESCALATING.
I SAT DOWN WITH MY FRIEND, *FREDDY DELUCA*, TO DISCUSS MY OPTIONS.
BRUNO, THE AIR NATIONAL GUARD IS THE ANSWER. SOONER OR LATER, YOU'RE GONNA GET DRAFTED, AND YOU CAN FORGET ABOUT TRAINING, COMPETING, OR YOUR APPRENTICESHIP.
WHAT'S INVOLVED?
FOUR MONTHS OF BASIC, THEN TWO DAYS A MONTH 'TIL YOUR HITCH IS UP.
I TOOK THE ADVICE, AND I WAS OFF TO LACKLAND AIRFORCE BASE IN SAN ANTONIO, TEXAS, FOR BASIC TRAINING TO BECOME A MEDIC.
YOU ARE A *MOUNTAIN*, SON. WHY ARE YOU A MEDIC?!? WHY ARE WE *WASTING* THIS MAN AS A MEDIC?!?
AND, JUST LIKE THAT, I WAS TRANSFERRED INTO THE AIR POLICE.

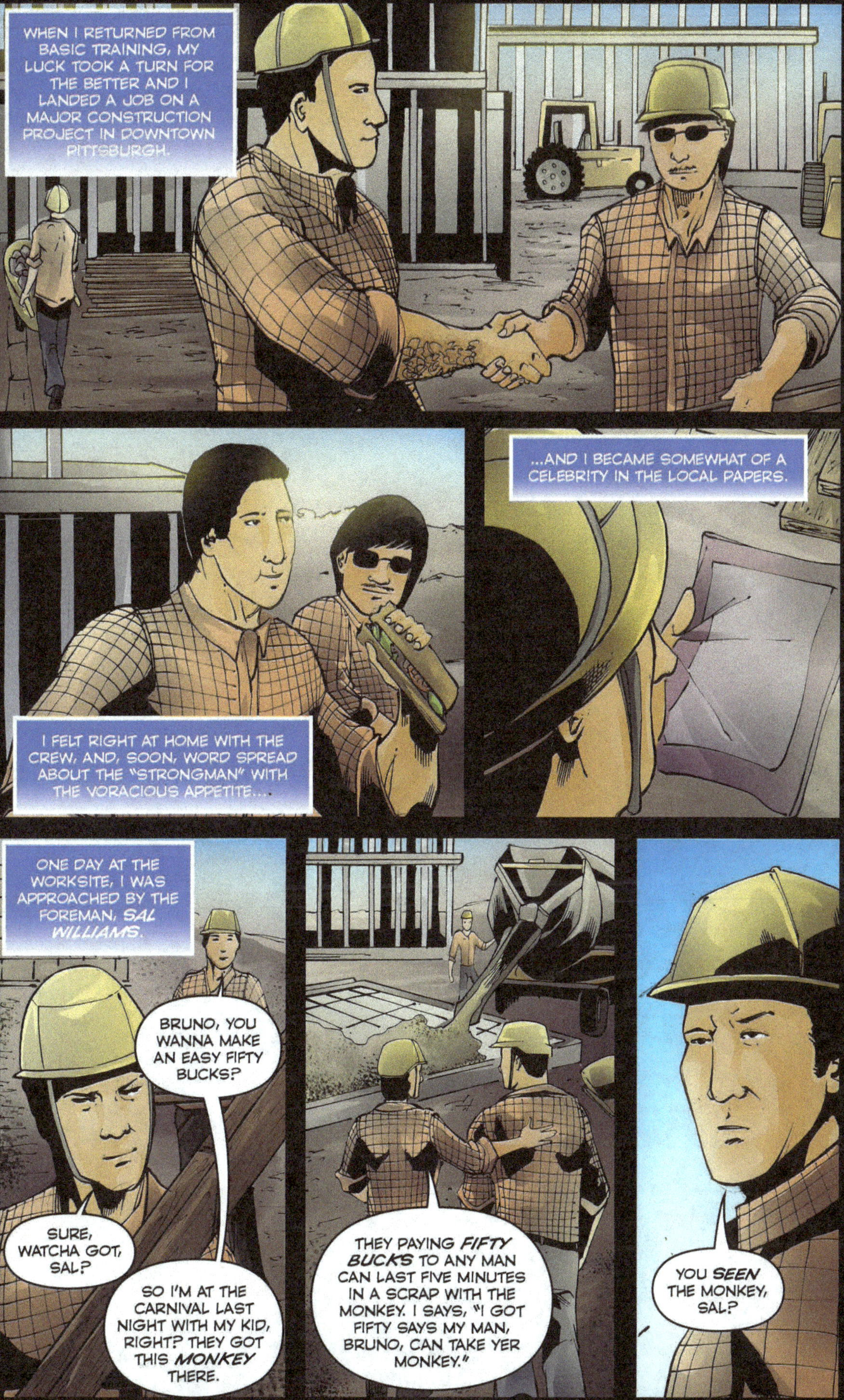

WHEN I RETURNED FROM BASIC TRAINING, MY LUCK TOOK A TURN FOR THE BETTER AND I LANDED A JOB ON A MAJOR CONSTRUCTION PROJECT IN DOWNTOWN PITTSBURGH.

I FELT RIGHT AT HOME WITH THE CREW, AND, SOON, WORD SPREAD ABOUT THE "STRONGMAN" WITH THE VORACIOUS APPETITE...

...AND I BECAME SOMEWHAT OF A CELEBRITY IN THE LOCAL PAPERS.

THAT NIGHT, A BROAD-CAST ABOUT THE CARNIVAL MONKEY SHOWED A SMALL, SHIVERING 18-INCH MONKEY IN A CAGE. I HAD NO DOUBT I COULD TAKE *THAT* MONKEY.
BUT WHEN I ARRIVED AT THE CARNIVAL, I FOUND A LARGE, SHAKING CAGE AND HEARD ANGRY GRUNTS AND GROWLS.
WHAT HAPPENED TO YOUR HAND?
MONKEY'S GOT *TEETH*.
WHAT'S MAKING ALL THAT *RUCKUS* IN THAT CAGE?
THAT'S YOUR *OPPONENT*, SON.
TO BE CONTINUED.

World Wide Wrestling Federation

WWWF

In 1963, the ubiquitous National Wrestling Alliance (NWA) changed forever after Toots Mondt and Vincent J. McMahon, of Capitol Wrestling Corporation, disputed the transfer of the NWA title from The Nature Boy Buddy Rogers to Lou Thesz, a well-traveled but, in their eyes, unworthy and unmarketable champion. The pair of entertainment entrepeneurs formed the World Wide Wrestling Federation (WWWF), from their territory in the American Northeast. They christened Rogers the inaugural WWWF champion (via a fictitious tournament in Rio de Janeiro), but, in May, 1963, The Living Legend Bruno Sammartino summarily dispatched Rogers in 48 seconds to take the title, and he didn't let it go for eight storied years.

As television exercised an increasing hold on the reach of professional wrestling in the 1960's, McMahon took the larger role in managing the WWWF, and Mondt eventually sold his share to him in the mid-1960's, paving the way for Vincent K. McMahon, second son of Vincent J., to join the business in 1969 and to fully assume control of the promotion by 1971. Coinciding with the beginning of the younger McMahon's reign was the end of Sammartino's championship run in a stunning loss to Ivan Koloff. Sammartino regained the WWWF title in 1973 for another extended reign of more than three years that included some of the greatest matches ever televised.

The decade of the 1970's saw a tripling of television syndication revenues and an influx of talent beyond Sammartino, including Nikolai Volkoff, Antonio Inoki (who famously battled Muhammad Ali in 1976), and Superstar Billy Graham. In 1979, the WWWF was renamed by Vincent K. McMahon to be the World Wrestling Federation (WWF), and so officially began a golden era of wrestling.

The Iron Sheik

Hossein Khosrow Ali Vaziri

Born:	March 15, 1942 Tehran, Iran
Spouse:	Caryl (m. 1976)
Height:	6' 0"
Weight:	258 lbs
Career:	1961-2010

The young man who would become 1980's heat magnet, The Iron Sheik, rose from poverty in pre-Revolution Iran to compete on his country's Greco-Roman wrestling team as part of the 1968 Olympic games held in Mexico City. He later even served a stint as a bodyguard for the Shah of Iran.

The road to professional wrestling stardom in the United States began when he relocated there in 1971 and claimed the Greco-Roman Wrestling Championship of the Amateur Athletic Union. He parlayed that success into a position as assistant coach of the U.S. Olympic team for the 1972 Games in Munich and was soon thereafter approached by legendary wrestler and trainer, Vern Gagne, to enter the world of professional wrestling. The heel persona of The Iron Sheik developed in part from his own background and experiences, as well as from the Iranian Revolution occurring in the late 1970's. Drawing further inspiration from hardcore legend Edward Farhat who originally used The Sheik moniker, he plied the politics of the era, including the notorious Iran Hostage Crisis, to draw heat like few wrestlers of any generation.

After assorted jobs and championships in various National Wrestling Alliance (NWA) territories, The Iron Sheik began the first of several runs with the World Wrestling Federation (WWF) in 1979, with remarkable success. He defeated Bob Backlund to become the WWF World Heavyweight Champion in December, 1983, only to lose the title to Hulk Hogan the following month. With tag team partner, Nikolai Volkoff, he captured the WWF World Tag Team Championship from the U.S. Express at the inaugural Wrestlemania, and the pair successfully defended the belts versus The Killer Bees at Wrestlemania III, sparking a long and infamous feud with the interfering Hacksaw Jim Duggan. Those years of anti-American heat in collaboration with the great Nikolai Volkoff are perhaps the best remembered of his storied career.

Nikolai Volkoff

The Developmental Years

Born:	October 14, 1947 Split, Croatia
Died:	July 29, 2018 Glen Arm, MD
Spouse:	Lynn (m. 1970)
Height:	6' 4"
Weight:	313 lbs
Career:	1967-2018

Art by Nathan Smith

The 2005 WWE Hall of Famer, Nikolai Volkoff, began life as Josip Peruzovic in the Socialist Republic of Croatia, then a part of communist Yugoslavia. While much of his career was spent as a communist heel, the reality was that Josip descended from a lineage of anti-communist activists, including his grandfather, Ante Perozovic, who was murdered by communist thugs. Early in life, Josip longed to escape communism.

At the tender age of fourteen, he left home to train to be an electrician but with the ulterior motive of preparing himself for a life outside Croatia. He took lessons in judo and weightlifting, ultimately qualifying for the Yugoslavian Junior National Team in the latter sport, and he met profound success, reigning as Junior National Champion for three consecutive years from 1965-1967. Faced with impending mandatory military service, Josip seized an opportunity to escape during an international weightlifting competition in Austria.

Granted a rare passport, thanks in large measure to his lifting prowess, Josip made the journey to Vienna, where he met Russian wrestler, Mijo Ujevich. They quickly built a bond of trust, and Mijo began Josip's earliest training in the art of wrestling, telling him of the Canadian professional wrestling scene in the process. Despite leading the competition on its penultimate day, Josip went directly from the facility to the Canadian embassy, where he requested, and was granted, asylum. Canadian officials expedited his transport to Calgary, where, at just age seventeen, he began life anew.

NIKOLAI
writer John E. Crowther
@crowman1971
artist Dell Barras
@DellBarras
colorist Andrew Pate
@Andrew_Pate
editor/
designer Kevin LaPorte
@kevinlaporte

ZAGREB, CROATIA - 1886.
MY GRANDFATHER, ANTE TOMSEVIC...
....WAS AN HONORABLE MAN, A CHAMPION WEIGHTLIFTER...
...CAPTAIN OF THE ROYAL GUARD, AND BODYGUARD TO AUSTRO-HUNGARIAN EMPEROR, FRANZ JOSEF.

AN HONORABLE MAN, BUT AN ENEMY TO YUGOSLAVIAN COMMUNISTS.
ANTE?
DA.

ANTE TOMSCEVIC? CAPTAIN OF THE ROYAL GUARD? BODYGUARD TO THE *SWINE*, FRANZ JOSEF?
I AM *ANTE TOMSEVIC*, CAPTAIN OF THE ROYAL GUARD. *WHO* ARE YOU, AND *WHAT* DO YOU WANT?
WE ARE REPRESENTATIVES OF SAVEZ KOMUNISTA JUGOSLAVIJE. WE *DEMAND* YOU TO COME WITH US!
YOU WILL DEMAND *NOTHING*, AND I WILL DO *NO* SUCH THING!
THEN, YOU *WILL* DIE!

MY GRANDFATHER FOUGHT VALIANTLY, ULTIMATELY KILLING *EIGHT* OF HIS ASSAILANTS.

BUT, IN THE END, EVEN *HE* COULD NOT SURVIVE THIS BRUTAL ASSAULT BY THE COMMUNISTS.

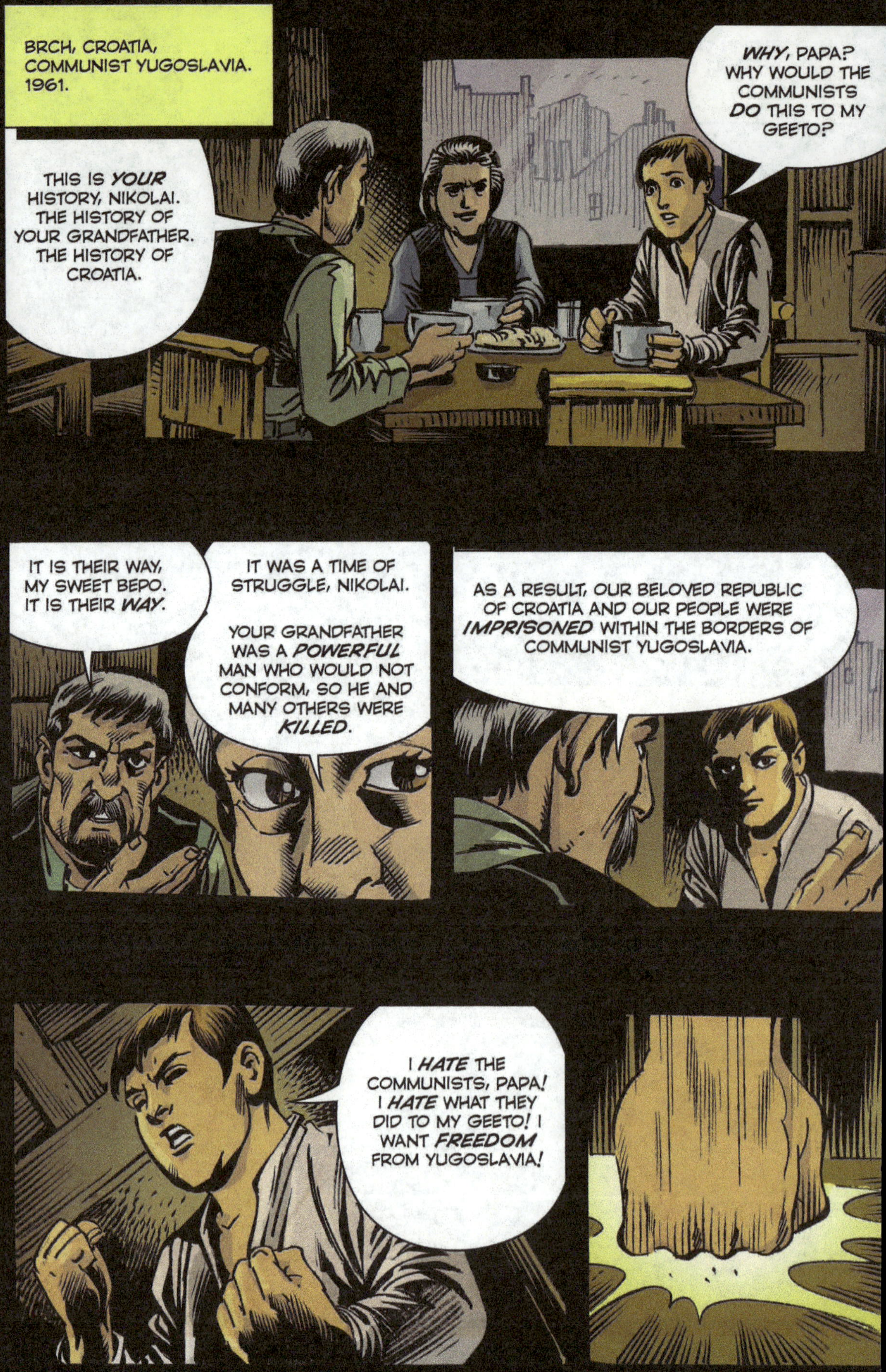

BRCH, CROATIA,
COMMUNIST YUGOSLAVIA.
1961.

THIS IS *YOUR* HISTORY, NIKOLAI. THE HISTORY OF YOUR GRANDFATHER. THE HISTORY OF CROATIA.

WHY, PAPA? WHY WOULD THE COMMUNISTS *DO* THIS TO MY GEETO?

EDUCATION AND SPORTS BRING FREEDOM, NIKOLAI. IF YOU WANT TO ESCAPE, YOU MUST FIRST GROW YOUR MIND. THEN, YOU MUST GROW YOUR BODY.
HERE? ON BRCH?
NO, NIKOLAI. YOU MUST LEAVE THE ISLAND. YOU MUST PURSUE YOUR SCHOOLING AND TRAINING IN THE CAPITOL.
THIS IS MY DREAM, PAPA, BUT I DON'T WANT TO LEAVE YOU AND MAMA ALONE. YOU NEED ME HERE.
FREEDOM FOR YOU WILL BE FREEDOM FOR ALL OF CROATIA, NIKOLAI.
THIS IS SOMETHING YOU MUST DO. GO TO THE AMERICAS AND TELL THE STORY OF THE CROATIAN PEOPLE.
YOU HAVE OUR BLESSINGS, SWEET BEPO.

AS THE AMERICANS LIBERATED EUROPE FROM THE EVILS OF THE NAZI REGIME, I, WITH THE BLESSINGS OF MY PARENTS, WOULD LIBERATE *MYSELF* FROM THE OPPRESSION OF COMMUNISM.

12

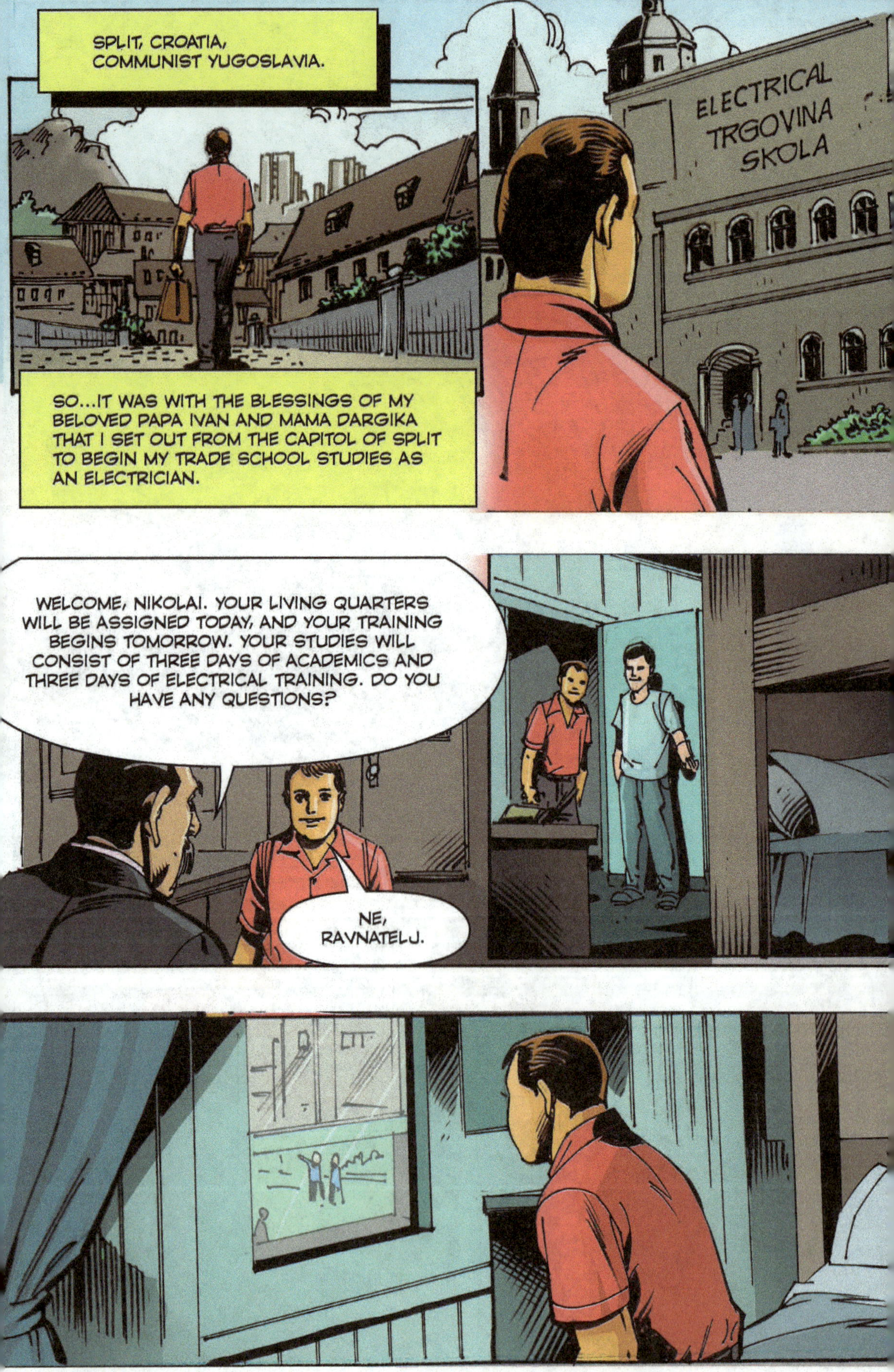

SPLIT, CROATIA,
COMMUNIST YUGOSLAVIA.

ELECTRICAL
TRGOVINA
SKOLA

SO...IT WAS WITH THE BLESSINGS OF MY BELOVED PAPA IVAN AND MAMA DARGIKA THAT I SET OUT FROM THE CAPITOL OF SPLIT TO BEGIN MY TRADE SCHOOL STUDIES AS AN ELECTRICIAN.

WITH THE MOVE TO SPLIT AT THE AGE OF FOURTEEN, MY SCHOOLING BEGAN. THREE DAYS OF MATH, SCIENCE, HISTORY, ART AND LANGUAGE...

...FOLLOWED BY THREE DAYS OF ELECTRICAL TRADE SCHOOL.

BUT, TO ESCAPE THE YOKE OF COMMUNISM, I NEEDED TO GROW *MORE* THAN MY MIND...I NEEDED TO ALSO GROW MY *BODY*. SO, I BEGAN MY TRAINING IN THE SPORT OF JUDO.
DŽUDO YUGOSLAVIA
I AM READY TO BEGIN MY TRAINING, SENSEI.
DA. HERE IS YOUR JUDOGI. YOU MAY JOIN THE CLASS.
TRAINING WAS NOT EASY...
...BUT, IT *WAS* REWARDING.

AND, TO HONOR MY GRANDFATHER ANTE, I BEGAN MY TRAINING AS A WEIGHTLIFTER, EVENTUALLY QUALIFYING FOR THE YUGOSLAVIAN JUNIOR NATIONAL TEAM.
GURNITE GA, NIKOLAI!
CESTITAM, NIKOLAI. YOU HAVE QUALIFIED FOR THE JUNIOR NATIONAL TEAM.

AND MY TRAINING WAS FRUITFUL, EARNING ME THE TITLE OF YUGOSLAVIAN JUNIOR NATIONAL CHAMPION FOR THREE CONSECUTIVE YEARS.
YOUR JUNIOR NATIONAL CHAMPION FOR 1965...JOSIP NIKOLAI PERUZOVIC!
AND THE 1966 YUGOSLAVIAN JUNIOR NATIONAL CHAMPION IS...JOSIP NIKOLAI PERUZOVIC VOLKOFF!
AND, FOR THE THIRD CONSECUTIVE YEAR...YOUR 1967 JUNIOR NATIONAL CHAMPION...JOSIP NIKOLAI PERUZOVIC VOLKOFF!

MILITARY SERVICE WOULD ***GREATLY*** DELAY MY ABILITY TO DEPART COMMUNIST YUGOSLAVIA. I NEEDED TO ***ESCAPE*** BEFORE I WAS CALLED TO SERVICE...

THE JUNIOR NATIONAL WEIGHTLIFTING TEAM WAS MY *VEHICLE*, AND AN UPCOMING INTERNATIONAL WEIGHT-LIFTING COMPETITION IN AUSTRIA WAS MY *OPPORTUNITY*.
IF I COULD CONVINCE MY COACHES AND THE REGISTER OF CITIZENS, I *MIGHT* SUCCEED.
NIKOLAI, YOU ARE OUR STRONGEST COMPETITOR. A STRONG SHOWING AT *THIS* EVENT WILL ELEVATE YOU IN THE EYES OF THE STATE.
COACH, I FEEL I'M READY. *THREE* CONSECUTIVE YEARS AS JUNIOR NATIONAL CHAMPION. I WANT TO COMPETE INTERNATIONALLY, BUT I NEED APPROVAL FROM THE REGISTRAR.
I'LL SEE WHAT I CAN DO.
HVALA.

WITH THE BACKING OF MY COACHES, I SET OUT TO REQUEST THAT THE REGISTRAR ISSUE ME A PASSPORT TO COMPETE IN AUSTRIA. PASSPORTS WERE *NOT* EASILY OBTAINED IN YUGOSLAVIA DURING THE COLD WAR, BUT, IF GRANTED, A YUGOSLAVIAN PASSPORT WAS CONSIDERED ONE OF THE MOST *CONVENIENT* IN THE EASTERN BLOC, ALLOWING ITS HOLDER TO TRAVEL FREELY BETWEEN THE EAST AND THE WEST.
REGISTAR GRADANA
MR. VOLKOFF, PLEASE BE SEATED.
I HAVE REVIEWED YOUR FILE, MR. VOLKOFF. YOU HAVE ACCOMPLISHED *MUCH* WITH OUR JUNIOR NATIONAL WEIGHTLIFTING TEAM. THIS IS AN EXCELLENT OPPORTUNITY FOR YOU TO...SHALL WE SAY...EXPRESS OUR *SUPERIORITY* IN THE INTERNATIONAL ARENA.
YOUR PASSPORT HAS BEEN *APPROVED*.
REPRESENT US WELL.

VIENNA, AUSTRIA. 1961.
S TERMINA

IT WAS IN VIENNA THAT I MET RUSSIAN WRESTLER, ***MIJO UJEVICH***. I EXPLAINED MY PLAN TO DEFECT TO THE WEST, AND MIJO QUICKLY TOOK ME UNDER HIS WING, TRAINING ME IN THE ART OF WRESTLING.

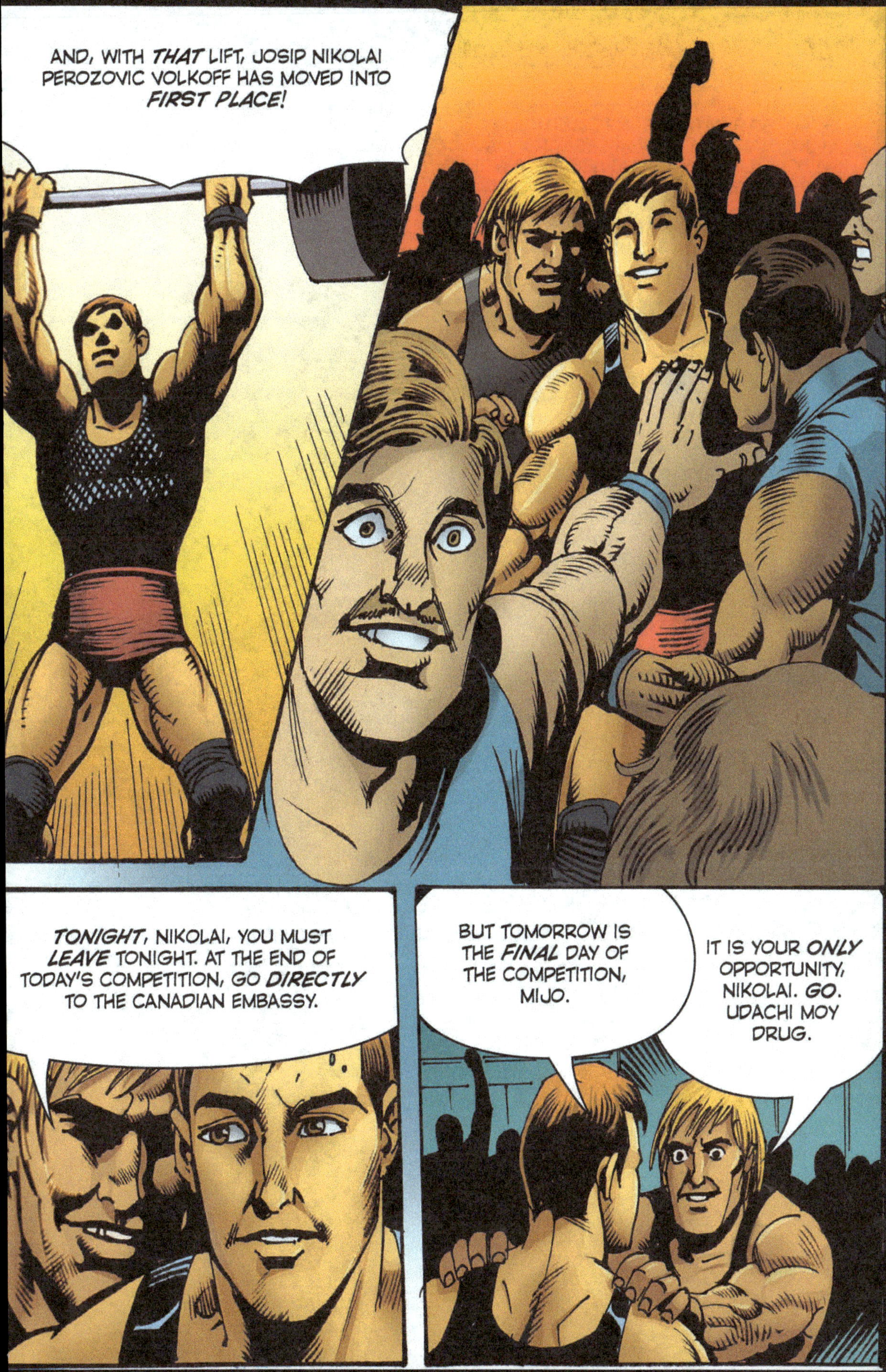

AND, WITH *THAT* LIFT, JOSIP NIKOLAI PEROZOVIC VOLKOFF HAS MOVED INTO *FIRST PLACE!*

SO, IT WAS WITH THE INSTRUCTIONS OF MIJO THAT I PLANNED MY ESCAPE. I WOULD *NOT* RETURN TO THE HOTEL, *NOR* WOULD I RETURN TO THE FINAL DAY OF COMPETITION IN THE MORNING. I WOULD GO DIRECTLY TO THE CANADIAN EMBASSY AND, HOPEFULLY, MY *NEW LIFE* IN THE WEST.
GYM

EMBASSY OF CANADA
MY NAME IS *JOSIP NIKOLAI PERUZOVIC VOLKOFF*, CITIZEN OF THE SOCIALIST REPUBLIC OF YUGOSLAVIA, AND I SEEK *ASYLUM*.
TO BE CONTINUED.

Randy Savage

The Macho Man

Born:	Nov. 15, 1952 Columbus, Ohio
Died:	May 20, 2011 Seminole, FL
Spouse:	Liz (m. 1984-92)
Height:	6' 2"
Weight:	237 lbs
Career:	1973-2005

Long before he became The Macho Man, young Randy Poffo was a high school baseball star in Downers Grove, Illinois. Drafted by the St. Louis Cardinals in 1971, he played in the minor leagues through 1974, until a shoulder injury and lack of progress toward the majors led him to the take the path of his father, Angelo Poffo, and his brother, Lanny, the path of professional wrestling that would change his life.

Randy and Lanny initially formed a tag team in the Pensacola, Florida-based Gulf Coast Wrestling and soon won the tag titles there. They found success throughout the National Wrestling Alliance (NWA) territories across the United States, until Angelo developed his own upstart wrestling promotion, International Championship Wrestling (ICW). The company heavily featured the brothers from 1979 through 1984 and it was during his time in ICW that Randy met and became involved with Liz Hulette, the woman who would become his first wife and his on-air valet, Miss Elizabeth.

Upon the dissolution of the ICW, Randy and Lanny joined their former business competitor, Jerry Lawler, in his Continential Wrestling Association (CWA) promotion based in Memphis, Tennessee. They continued there as a successful tag team, feuding with the Rock 'n' Roll Express, while Randy entered solo competition against Lawler himself, competing for the AWA Southern Heavyweight Championship from 1984-1985, until Randy ultimately lost a Loser Leaves Town match to Lawler.

Within a month of exiting CWA, Randy signed with the World Wrestling Federation (WWF) and quickly established Miss Elizabeth as his manager. Their jealousy and control gimmick fueled most of the feuds and storylines throughout his storied WWF career.

Randy Savage went on to legendary runs as WWF Intercontinental Champion (1985-87), King of the Ring (1987), and WWF Champion (1988-89). In 1989, he formed the Mega Powers tag team with Hulk Hogan, until the two feuded over Randy's jealousy of Hogan's relationship with Miss Elizabeth, culminating in Hogan defeating Savage for the WWF Championship at Wrestlemania V.

The 1990's brought a temporary retirement, including a job as WWF color commentator amidst occasional matches and feuds between injuries, before a last big run in World Championship Wrestling (WCW) following the expiration of his WWF contract in 1994.

A long-simmering feud with Ric Flair reignited in the WCW, and the two twice juggled the promotion's World Heavyweight Championship after Savage won it in the inaugural 60-man, three-ring battle royal in 1995. Though actually divorced by this time, Miss Elizabeth joined Randy in the WCW but soon turned on him in favor of Flair.

During the New World Order (nWo) era of WCW, Savage returned from a brief hiatus, due to a contract dispute, to team with Sting against the then-popular stable, only to quickly betray him and join the nWo. Randy soon defeated Sting to capture the WCW World Heavyweight Championship for a third time, later defending it, albeit unsuccessfully, against old rival, Hulk Hogan.

Injuries took their toll in the ensuing years, but he enjoyed a resurgent career as the marketing face of Slim Jims and as an actor, appearing in the first *Spider-Man* film. Randy Savage was posthumously inducted into the WWE Hall of Fame in 2015.

Miss Elizabeth

First Lady of Wrestling

Born:	Nov. 19, 1960 Frankfort, KY
Died:	May 1, 2003 Marietta, GA
Spouses:	Randy Savage Cary Lubetsky
Height:	5' 4"
Weight:	115 lbs
Career:	1983-2003

Elizabeth Ann Hulette earned a Bachelor's degree in Communications from the University of Kentucky and, in 1983, parlayed her education into a job as an announcer for Angelo Poffo's International Championship Wrestling (ICW) promotion.

During her tenure there, she became involved with Poffo's son, Randy Savage, and the two married in 1984.

When the ICW folded that same year, Elizabeth joined Randy as he elevated his career by moving to the World Wrestling Federation (WWF). She debuted as his manager, Miss Elizabeth, following a gimmick featuring established WWF managers competing to work with The Macho Man. For years following, the pair worked a jealousy angle during Savage's feuds with various other WWF wrestlers, including George "The Animal" Steele, The Honky Tonk Man, Ric Flair, and even Hulk Hogan, the latter incident famously splitting the Mega Powers tag team the Hulkster shared with Savage. Typically, the opposing wrestler implied that Miss Elizabeth wanted them more than she wanted Savage or acted to damage their relationship in some manner and Savage raged against both his wife and his enemy. The bit lasted many years and drove the pair to superstardom.

This managerial persona outlasted even their marriage, as they divorced in 1992, but she briefly returned as Savage's manager in World Championship Wrestling (WCW) in 1996, before turning on him a few weeks later, a frequent angle in the promotion

Lanny Poffo

The Genius

Born:	Dec. 28, 1958 Calgary, AB, CA
Height:	6' 0"
Weight:	252 lbs
Career:	1973-Present

Art by Rando Dixon

The son of Angelo Poffo, an accomplished pro wrestler and 1958 NWA Chicago United States Heavyweight Champion, as well as the brother of 2015 WWE Hall of Famer, The Macho Man Randy Savage, Lanny Poffo eschewed a potential baseball career in favor of an early decision to follow his father's path to the squared circle. Angelo personally oversaw his young son's training in all aspects of the wrestling business, culminating in a 1973 debut match between the two in Kentucky's All-Star Wrestling.

From that inital loss to his own father, Lanny successfully challenged for the All-South Wrestling Georgia Junior Heavyweight Championship against Ted Oates and teamed with Angelo to win the National Wrestling Alliance (NWA) Tag Team Championship from Bobo Brazil and "Flying" Fred Curry. Upon his brother's decision to leave professional baseball, Lanny and Randy teamed in Pensacola, Florida's Gulf Coast Wrestling promotion, where they defeated the original British Bulldogs to capture the NWA Gulf Coast Championship.

In 1978, the brothers and their father collaborated to form their own promotion, International Championship Wrestling (ICW), which flourished through 1984, when it merged with Jerry Lawler's Continental Wrestling Association (CWA). Randy soon signed with the World Wrestling Federation (WWF), and Lanny followed as "Leaping" Lanny, renowned for hurling poem-inscribed frisbees into the audience before matches. In 1989, he adopted the heel persona of "The Genius" and memorably aligned with Mr. Perfect and feuded with Hulk Hogan and other 1980's luminaries.

writer	John E. Crowther @crowman1971	colorist	Andrew Pate @Andrew_Pate
artist pp. 55-69	Randolph Dixon @RandoDixonArt	letterer	Jayson Kretzer @JaysonKretzer
artist pp. 70-85	Alan McMillian @Alan_McMillian	editor/ designer	Kevin LaPorte @kevinlaporte
inker pp. 67-69	Amanda Rachels @AmandaRachels		

APRIL 15, 1989
BEHOLD THE WORLD'S SMARTEST MAN
SO MASCULINE AND PROUD.
THE EPITOME OF GENIUS
AMAZINGLY ENDOWED.
A ONE-MAN WRESTLING RENAISSANCE.
JUST LET YOUR HEART REJOICE.
AND BATHE IN ALL THE LUXURY
OF MY POETIC VOICE.
THE BEST OF MY COMPETITORS
ARE SO INFERIOR.
I FAR OUTTHINK THEIR GREATEST THOUGHTS
WITH MY POSTERIOR.
AND WHEN THE BELL HAS SOUNDED
ON MY STUNNING VICTORY
I'LL VIEW THAT MESSY SPOT
WHERE MY OPPONENT USED TO BE.
THE ARISTOCRATIC PLEASURE
OF INFLICTING SO MUCH PAIN
GIVES RISE TO SO MUCH PASSION
IT IS BORDERLINE INSANE.
ALTHOUGH MY VERSE MAY SEEM PERVERSE
TO EVERY FOE AND FAN
I'M STILL THE GENIUS LANNY POFFO--
THE WORLD'S SMARTEST MAN.

DOWNERS GROVE, ILLINOIS --1970
PROFESSIONAL WRESTLING WASN'T ALWAYS THE PLAN.
GROWING UP IN DOWNERS GROVE, ILLINOIS, MY OLDER BROTHER **RANDY POFFO**, LATER TO BE KNOWN AS **RANDY SAVAGE**, WAS A HIGH SCHOOL BASEBALL STAR.
RANDY-- YOU'RE UP! LANNY., ON DECK!
I, ON THE OTHER HAND, WASN'T FIT TO **FLUSH.**
RANDY WAS A STAR--
--AND **DOMINANT** ON THE HIGH SCHOOL FIELD--
--BUT I KNEW FROM WATCHING BIG LEAGUERS, LIKE **JERRY MUMPHREY**, THAT RANDY WASNOT DESTINED FOR PROFESSIONAL BASEBALL STARDOM.

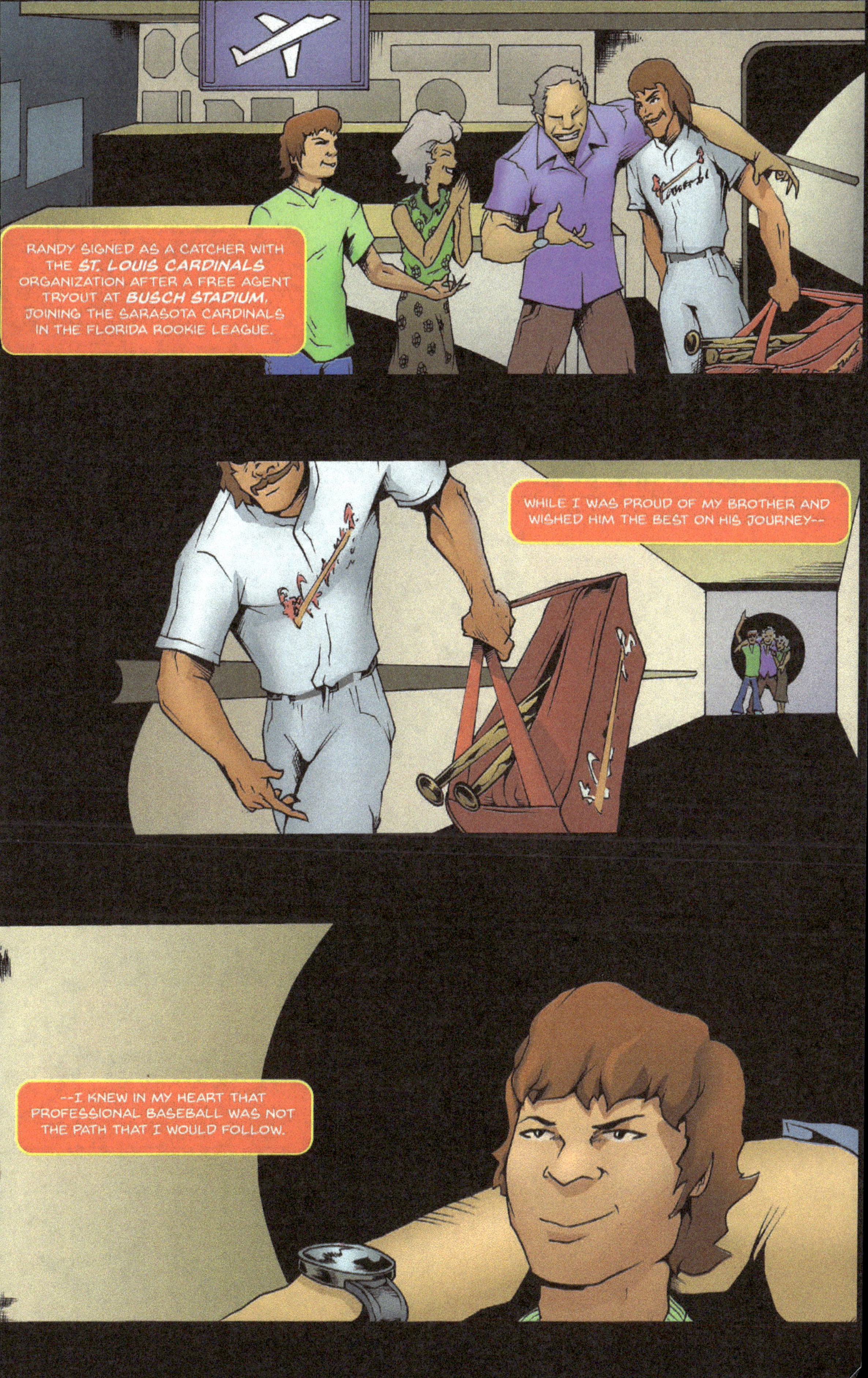
RANDY SIGNED AS A CATCHER WITH THE ST. LOUIS CARDINALS ORGANIZATION AFTER A FREE AGENT TRYOUT AT BUSCH STADIUM, JOINING THE SARASOTA CARDINALS IN THE FLORIDA ROOKIE LEAGUE.
WHILE I WAS PROUD OF MY BROTHER AND WISHED HIM THE BEST ON HIS JOURNEY--
--I KNEW IN MY HEART THAT PROFESSIONAL BASEBALL WAS NOT THE PATH THAT I WOULD FOLLOW.

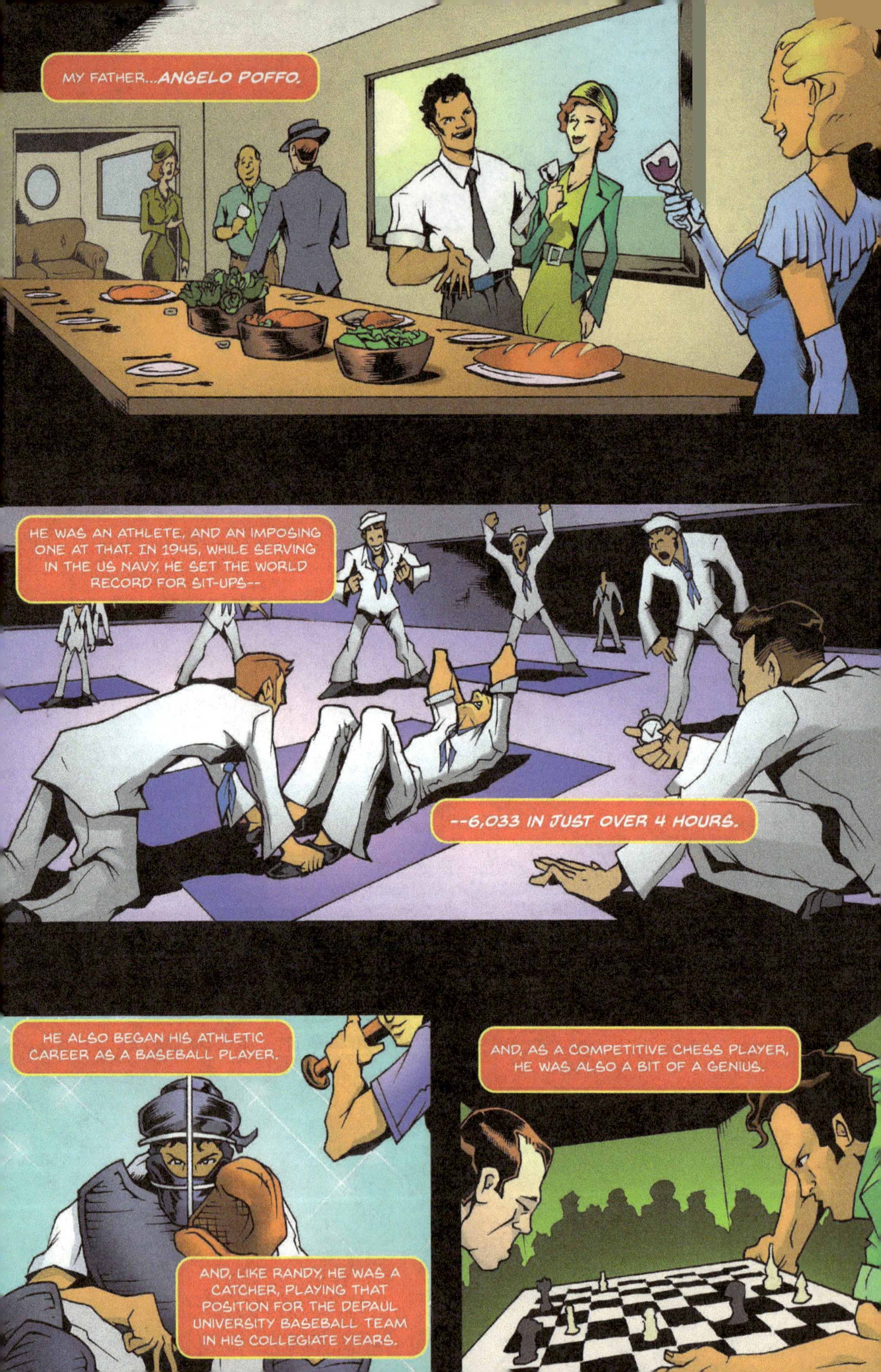
MY FATHER...ANGELO POFFO.
HE WAS AN ATHLETE, AND AN IMPOSING ONE AT THAT. IN 1945, WHILE SERVING IN THE US NAVY, HE SET THE WORLD RECORD FOR SIT-UPS--
--6,033 IN JUST OVER 4 HOURS.
HE ALSO BEGAN HIS ATHLETIC CAREER AS A BASEBALL PLAYER.
AND, LIKE RANDY, HE WAS A CATCHER, PLAYING THAT POSITION FOR THE DEPAUL UNIVERSITY BASEBALL TEAM IN HIS COLLEGIATE YEARS.
AND, AS A COMPETITIVE CHESS PLAYER, HE WAS ALSO A BIT OF A GENIUS.

Believe It or Not! by Ripley

JOHN HEAD
MAL FOOT
RALPH HAND
HERB FINGER
ALL WORK IN THE
ME BUILDING
New York

MY DAD WAS IN THE NAVY,
AS HISTORY WILL TELL.
AS HE WAS BLEEDING THROUGH THE
MATS, A WORLD RECORD FELL.

HE DID 6,000 SIT UPS
WITH AN EXTRA 33,
TO GLORIFY OUR SAVIOR
WHO DIED ON CALVARY.

AND ROBERT RIPLEY'S FEATURE
CELEBRATED THIS EVENT,
GIVING CREDENCE TO "SUCCESS
IS NOT AN ACCIDENT."

ZINO
FRANCESCATTI
PLAYS 2800 NOTES
IN LESS THAN 4 MINUTES!
"Perpetuum Mobile"
by Paganni

SINGING SQUIRREL
Owned by
L.R. CONNER, Collinston, La.

THAT'S ALWAYS BEEN HIS MOTTO
THROUGH TIMES BOTH GOOD AND BAD.
HE'S A REAL HALL OF FAMER AND THE
WORLD'S GREATEST DAD.

ANGELO POFFO DID 6,033 CONSECUTIVE SIT-UPS!
Downers Grove, Ill.

BUT IT WAS AS A PROFESSIONAL WRESTLER THAT MY FATHER WAS MOST FAMOUSLY KNOWN, BEGINNING HIS CAREER IN THE LATE-40'S IN ILLINOIS, AND WINNING SEVERAL TITLES, INCLUDING---
---THE NWA-CHICAGO UNITED STATES HEAVYWEIGHT CHAMPIONSHIP IN 1958--
AND THE WWA TAG TEAM CHAMPIONSHIP WITH *NICOLI VOLKOFF* IN 1964.
CCCP
I WANTED TO FOLLOW THE PATH OF PROFESSIONAL WRESTLING, AND WHO BETTER TO LEAD ME ON THIS JOURNEY THAN MY FATHER--THE GREAT *ANGELO POFFO*.

DAD, I WANT TO BE A PROFESSIONAL WRESTLER.
WHAT ABOUT YOUR BASEBALL CAREER, SON?
I DON'T SEE MYSELF AS A BASEBALL PLAYER, DAD. I WANT TO WRESTLE. AND I WANT YOU TO TRAIN ME.
IF THAT'S WHAT YOU WANT.
BUT REMEMBER, ONCE YOUR TRAINING STARTS, IT NEVER ENDS. A PROFESSIONAL WRESTLER NEVER STOPS LEARNING.
MEET ME AT THE GYM AT 5:00 A.M.--
--DON'T BE LATE.

AND SO MY TRAINING BEGAN.
THE ART OF PROFESSIONAL WRESTLING ISN'T MASTERED SOLELY THROUGH EXERCISE---
---VERBAL INSTRUCTION---
---OR WRITTEN INSTRUCTION.
THE MASTERY IS ALSO OBTAINED THROUGH COUNTLESS HOURS OF WATCHING OTHERS PERFORM---

---AND IN-RING EXPERIENCE.

LATER THAT YEAR, I TRAVELED TO THE STATE OF KENTUCKY--
WELCOME TO
KENTUCKY
THE BLUEGRASS STATE
EVERY THURSDAY NIGHT IS WRESTLING NIGHT IN PADUCAH
WITH PHIL GOLDEN'S ALL-STAR WRESTLING
PADUCAH SPORTS ARENA 1025 KENTUCKY AVENUE
THURSDAY NIGHT, SEPTEMBER 13TH, 1973
BIGGEST GRUDGE BATTLE OF THE YEAR
WORLD TAG TEAM BELTS AT STAKE
—MAIN EVENT—
Buddy Hock & Paul Christy
Managed By Saul Weingeroff
VS.
Karl & Kurt Vonbrauner
World Champions Managed By Windell Burchett
(2 Out Of 3 Falls To A Finish)
Saul Wants Revenge For What The Germans Did To Him On TV.
The Graduate vs. Prof. Gary Parlor
Princess Natasha vs. Sherri Lee
To Wrestle Sarah McKay For Title
Angello Poffo vs. Leaping Lannie
315 Broadway
386
$3.00
Adult General $2.50
Child General $1.50
8:30 P.M.
Watch All-Star Wrestling With Buzz Benton announcing on Channel 29 Sat. at 4:30 & WSIL Harrisburg Saturday Night After Late Movie.
--WHERE I DEBUTED WITH PHIL GOLDEN'S ALL-STAR WRESTLING AGAINST MY FATHER, ANGELO POFFO.
IN MY FIRST PUBLIC MATCH, I SQUARED OFF AGAINST MY FATHER.
ALTHOUGH IT WASN'T A WIN IN THE RECORD BOOK--
--I LEARNED GREATLY FROM THE PERFORMANCE.
--AND YOUR WINNER... BY PIN-FALL-- ANGELO POFFO!

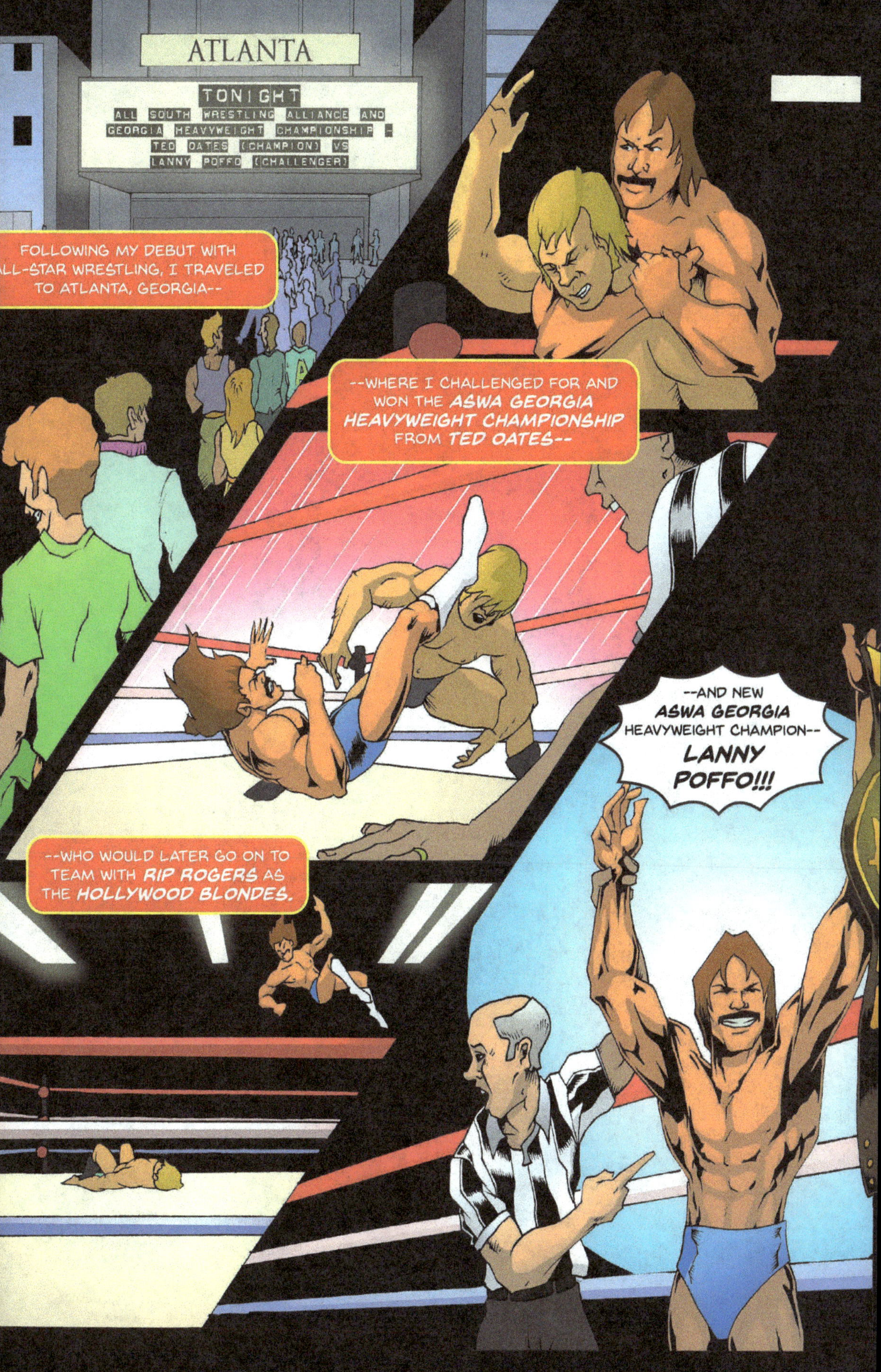
ATLANTA
TONIGHT
ALL SOUTH WRESTLING ALLIANCE AND
GEORGIA HEAVYWEIGHT CHAMPIONSHIP -
TED OATES (CHAMPION) VS
LANNY POFFO (CHALLENGER)
FOLLOWING MY DEBUT WITH ALL-STAR WRESTLING, I TRAVELED TO ATLANTA, GEORGIA--
--WHERE I CHALLENGED FOR AND WON THE ASWA GEORGIA HEAVYWEIGHT CHAMPIONSHIP FROM TED OATES--
--WHO WOULD LATER GO ON TO TEAM WITH RIP ROGERS AS THE HOLLYWOOD BLONDES.
--AND NEW ASWA GEORGIA HEAVYWEIGHT CHAMPION-- LANNY POFFO!!!

WHILE APPEARING FOR ALL-SOUTH WRESTLING IN ATLANTA, I WAS ALSO MAKING APPEARANCES FOR BIG TIME WRESTLING, OUT OF DETROIT, MICHIGAN--
--WHERE MY FATHER AND I CAPTURED THE NWA WORLD TAG TEAM CHAMPIONSHIP FROM BOBO BRAZIL AND "FLYING" FRED CURRY.

IN 1975, RANDY WAS RELEASED FROM HIS PROFESSIONAL BASEBALL CONTRACT AND HE JOINED ME IN *PENSACOLA, FLORIDA,* WHERE I WAS COMPETING WITH GULF COAST WRESTLING.
RANDY HAD BEEN MAKING SPORADIC WRESTLING APPEARANCES DURING THE BASEBALL OFF SEASON, OFTEN TIMES AS A REFEREE, TO LEARN THE TRADE IN ANTICIPATION OF A FUTURE CAREER IN THE BUSINESS.
BUT NOW RANDY HAD WALKED AWAY FROM BASEBALL AND HIS FUTURE IN WRESTLING WAS TRULY ABOUT TO BEGIN.
I'M READY.
YOU NEED TRAINING, RANDY. LIKE I TOLD LANNY, YOU ARE CONSTANTLY LEARNING IN THIS INDUSTRY.
YOU NEED RING TIME. LET'S PAIR THE TWO OF YOU UP AS ***A TAG TEAM.***

AND SO, WE FORMED A TAG TEAM IN GULF COAST WRESTLING AND WERE SLATED TO FACE--
--THE TEAM OF ENGLISH WRESTLERS JOHN FOLEY AND TED HEATH, THE ORIGINAL "BRITISH BULLDOGS"--
--FOR THE NWA GULF COAST TAG TEAM CHAMPIONSHIP--
--WHICH WE WON WITH AMAZING FLAIR!

IN 1978, AFTER SEVERAL SUCCESSFUL YEARS WRESTLING THROUGHOUT THE VARIOUS NWA TERRITORIES, RANDY AND I RETURNED TO KENTUCKY TO MEET WITH OUR FATHER.
WE WERE READY TO BREAK AWAY FROM THE NWA AND CREATE OUR OWN PROMOTION--
ICW
--INTERNATIONAL CHAMPIONSHIP WRESTLING, OR, ICW, WHICH WOULD COMPETE WITH THE NWA TERRITORIES FROM 1979 UNTIL 1984, AND WOULD FOLD SHORTLY AFTER RANDY AND I LEFT THE ORGANIZATION FOR THE WWF.
ICW

ICW
INTERCONTINENTAL CHAMPIONSHIP WRESTLING
THE ICW ROSTER WAS LOADED WITH TALENT, INCLUDING SUCH STARS AS RON GARVIN--
--OX BAKER AND PEZ WHATLEY--
--BOB ORTON, JR.--
--AND CRUSHER BROOMFIELD, LATER TO BE KNOWN AS THE ONE MAN GANG AND AKEEM.

BUT UNDOUBTEDLY, THE STARS OF THE PROMOTION WERE ME--
--AND YOUR ICW WORLD HEAVYWEIGHT CHAMPION-- LANNY POFFO!!!
--HOLDING THE ICW WORLD HEAVYWEIGHT CHAMPIONSHIP THREE TIMES, INCLUDING BECOMING THE FINAL ICW HEAVYWEIGHT CHAMPION ON MAY 10, 1978--
--AND RANDY, WHO HAD ADOPTED THE NAME RANDY SAVAGE, AND ALSO HELD THE ICW WORLD HEAVYWEIGHT TITLE ON SEPARATE OCCASIONS--
--AND WHO HAD BEGUN A ROMANCE WITH ICW ON-CAMERA HOSTESS, LIZ HULETTE--LATER TO BE KNOWN TO WRESTLING FANS AS MISS ELIZABETH.
ICW
OOH YEAH!

CWA
THROUGHOUT THESE YEARS, THE ICW WAS IN DIRECT COMPETITION WITH ANOTHER WRESTLING ORGANIZATION BASED IN KENTUCKY AND TENNESSEE--THE CWA, OR CONTINENTAL WRESTLING ASSOCIATION, RUN BY JERRY JARRET AND JERRY LAWLER.
THE CWA, AS AN NWA AND LATER AWA AFFILIATE, WAS ALSO HOME TO MANY WRESTLING GREATS, INCLUDING JERRY LAWLER--
--BRUISER BRODY, AND RICK RUDE.
BUT IN 1984, THE TWO ORGANIZATIONS REACH
AN AGREEMENT, BRINGING ALL OF THESE
SUPERSTARS TOGETHER UNDER ONE BANNER

IT WAS FOLLOWING THE MERGER OF ICW AND THE CWA THAT RANDY CAUGHT THE ATTENTION OF A CERTAIN INDIVIDUAL--AN INDIVIDUAL THAT WOULD CHANGE BOTH OF OUR LIVES FOREVER.
THAT MAN WAS GEORGE SCOTT, A DRIVING FORCE BEHIND THE WORLD WRESTLING FEDERATION, OR WWF, LATER TO BECOME THE WWE.
RANDY WAS A STAR WITH IMMEASURABLE CHARISMA. HE HAD GRASPED THE ATTENTION OF SCOTT, WHO WAS POISED TO MAKE AN OFFER.
RANDY-- I WANT TO BRING THE MACHO MAN TO THE WWF.
INTERESTING PROPOSITION GEORGE-- EMM HUH. BUT I GOT A PROPOSITION FOR YOU TOO, YEAH. I'M BRINGIN' MY BROTHER LANNY WITH ME, DIG IT!?!
YEAH--
I DIG IT.

JUNE 21, 1985.
MADISON SQUARE GARDEN.
WRESTLING AS "LEAPING" LANNY POFFO, I MADE MY WWF DEBUT AGAINST TERRY GIBBS.
--AND SOMEBODY WITH THIS MAN'S CREDENTIALS, IT WAS JUST A MATTER OF TIME.
ABSOLUTELY.
I OPENED THE MATCH BY WOWING THE CROWD WITH MY LEAPING ABILITIES.
--AND, AFTER GIBBS TOOK THE FIGHT OUTSIDE THE RING WITH HIS UNDERHANDED TACTICS--
--I CLOSED OUT THE BATTLE, TO THE AMAZEMENT OF ALL IN AUDIENCE, WITH A PERFECTLY EXECUTED BACKFLIP OFF THE TOP ROPE--
--FOR THE PIN.
MY FIRST VICTORY IN THE WWF.

IN THE AUTUMN OF 1985, FOLLOWING MY VICTORY AT MADISON SQUARE GARDEN, I MADE AN APPEARANCE ON TUESDAY NIGHT TITANS---A SHOW HOSTED BY VINCE MCMAHON AND CO-HOSTED BY LORD AWFUL HAYES. IT WAS HERE THAT I RECITED MY FIRST POEM FOR THE WRESTLING UNIVERSE AND ESTABLISHED MYSELF AS A "BABYFACE"
LADIES AND GENTLEMAN ---"LEAPING LANNY POPPO".
I'M NOT YOUR AVERAGE WRESTLER, BUT I WOULDN'T WANT TO BE. I NEVER SCREAM OR KISS MY ARMS, I'M HAPPY JUST BEING ME.
I CALL MYSELF "LEAPING LANNY", I VALIDATE WHAT I SAY. TO EVERY SINGLE WRESTLING FAN, THAT'S WATCHNG USA.
YES I BELIEVE IN MIRACLES, AS GOD HAS BLESSED THIS GREAT LAND. I BELIEVE THE REFEREE, WILL SOON BE RAISING MY HAND!
GEORGE SCOTT LOVED THE POEM. IT WAS A HIT AND WOULD REMAIN MY GIMMICK THROUGHOUT MY CAREER.
THAT WAS MARVELOUS, LANNY! ROM NOW ON, I WANT YOU RECITE A POEM BEFORE EVERY MATCH.
BUT I DIDN'T WANT TO MERELY RECITE MY POETRY. I WANTED TO PUT MY POEMS IN THE HANDS OF MY FANS.
SO--TAKING A CUE FROM THE FABULOUS KANGAROOS TAG TEAM, WHO WOULD TOSS CARDBOARD BOOMERANGS TO THE CROWD, I WOULD WRITE MY POETRY ON FRISBEES, TO BE THROWN TO MY FANS BEFORE MATCHES.

BY 1987, I WAS AN ESTABLISHED BABYFACE WITH THE FANS. THE CROWDS LOVED "LEAPING" LANNY POFFO--THE POET LAUREATE OF THE WORLD WRESTLING FEDERATION.
BUT THE COMPANY NEEDED A SACRIFICIAL LAMB.
THE WWF HAD DECIDED TO TURN ANDRE THE GIANT INTO A HEEL AND WANTED TO BUILD ANDRE'S HEEL STATUS PRIOR TO HIS SHOWDOWN WITH HULK HOGAN AT WRESTLEMANIA III.
SO I SAT DOWN FOR A MEETING WITH GEORGE, ANDRE AND GORILLA MONSOON.
LANNY--- WE NEED TO MAKE ANDRE UNPOPULAR WITH THE FANS. THERE'S ONLY ONE MAN FOR THE JOB.
CAN YOU AND WILL YOU GIVE BLOOD FOR ANDRE?
I'LL DO IT.
DON'T MAKE A MONKEY OUT OF ME.
I CAN'T MAKE A MONKEY OUT O A GORILLA.

THE SCENE WAS SET. A BATTLE ROYALE ON LIVE TELEVISION. MARCH 14, 1987. SATURDAY NIGHT MAIN EVENT.
ANDRE CAME AT ME ALMOST FROM THE MOMENT THE BELL RANG AND HAMMERED ME WITH A HEAD BUTT, WHICH BURST MY HEAD OPEN IN A SPRAY OF CRIMSON.
HE THEN TOSSED ME FROM THE RING---
---WHERE I LANDED IN A POOL OF MY OWN BLOOD---
I HAD DONE MY JOB.
ANDRE'S HEEL TURN WAS COMPLETE.

IN THE BEGINNING OF 1989, I FELT THAT MY CHARACTER HAD BECOME STALE, SO I NEEDED SOMETHING NEW, AND FELT THAT A HEEL TURN ON MY PART WOULD BE THE ANSWER.
SO I MET WITH MY FRIEND AND LONG-TIME RING ANNOUNCER, HOWARD FINKLE, TO CREATE MY CHARACTER, THE GENIUS.
LET'S CONTINUE WITH YOUR POETRY, BUT YOU SHOULD NOW USE IT TO RIDICULE AND TAUNT YOUR BABYFACE OPPONENTS. BELITTLE THEM AND THE CROWDS, WHILE YOU BRAG ABOUT YOUR INTELLECT.
THAT'S GENIUS!
I EXPLAINED MY PLAN TO TURN HEEL TO SEVERAL OF MY PEERS, ONE OF WHICH WAS JAY STRONGBOW
YOU'LL NEVER MAKE IT AS A HEEL, LANNY. YO'URE TOO DAMN GOOD LOOKIN'.
YEAH, JAY? WELL-- YOU'RE ONE OF THE UGLIEST GUYS I KNOW AND YOU'RE A BABYFACE.

MARCH 18, 1989.
BOSTON GARDEN.
ON MARCH 18, 1989, BEFORE A CAPACITY CROWD IN BOSTON GARDEN--
--I MADE MY HEEL TURN BY INSULTING THE BOSTON CROWD.
MY NAME IS LANNY POFFO, I ALWAYS KNOW WHAT'S UP. THE BRUINS HAVEN'T GOT A CHANCE, TO WIN THE STANLEY CUP.
THE RED SOX HAVEN'T WON IN YEARS, I HOPE THEY NEVER DO. THE CELTICS ARE A TRAVESTY THE PATRIOTS ARE TOO.

FOLLOWING A SERIES OF TELEVISED VIGNETTES TO ESTABLISH MY GENIUS CHARACTER, I BEGAN WRESTLING APPEARANCES.
I WOULD BERATE THE CROWDS WITH MY POETRY--
--TAUNT MY OPPONENTS WITH MY FLAMBOYANT MANNERISMS--
---AND AGGRAVATE WRESTLING FANS, REFEREES AND MY OPPONENTS BY CREATING AND SOLVING MATHEMATICAL EQUATIONS DURING MY MATCHES THUS TILTING THE MATCHES IN FAVOR.
$5\int a^2x^6dx$
$(a^u)'=a^u \ln a\, u'$
$(\ln x)'=\frac{1}{x}(x>0)$
=WIN!

ON NOVEMBER 25, 1989, WHILE SERVING AS "ADVISOR" TO WRESTLER MR. PERFECT, MY MOMENT AS THE GENIUS HAD ARRIVED. I WOULD FACE HULK HOGAN ON SATURDAY NIGHT MAIN EVENT FOR THE WORLD HEAVYWEIGHT CHAMPIONSHIP.
THERE'S ONLY ONE MAN SMART ENOUGH TO TAKE HULK HOGAN DOWN, THE GENIUS HAS A DEVASTATING PLAN. YOU'RE LOOKING AT THE FUTURE WORLD WRESTLING FEDERATION, WHO APPEALS TO THE MODERN THINKING MAN.
WHEN I EMERGE VICTORIOUS WITH GOLD AROUND MY WAIST, I SHALL BE THE MOST SPLENDIFEROUS OF ALL. DON'T TELL ME HULK IS 6'8" AND I'M JUST 6'2", BETWEEN THE EARS I'M OVER 10' TALL.
HE WANTS TO WRAP HIS 24" PYTHONS AROUND MY NECK AND GIVE HIS FAMOUS "WHACHA GONNA DO?". BY THE POWER OF THE GENIUS AND THE WORLD'S SMARTEST MAN, I'LL RELY ON MY INCREDIBLE IQ.
HA! HEMMINGWAY AND FROST---THEY AIN'T GOT NOTHIN' ON THIS GUY.

THE MATCH PROCEEDED ACCORDING TO PLAN, WITH ME TAUNTING THE CHAMPION AND THE CROWD WITH MY UNORTHODOX MOVES AND INTELLECTUAL PROWESS.

SLAP!
WHEN HOGAN CROSSED THE LINE AND TOSSED ME OVER THE TOP ROPE TO THE FLOOR BELOW--
--MR. PERFECT CAME TO MY AID--
--DISTRACTING THE CHAMPION--

--AND HELPING ME EARN THE VICTORY, ALBEIT NOT THE CHAMPIONSHIP.
THE WINNER OF THIS MATCH, AS THE RESULT OF A COUNT OUT ---THE GENIUS!!!
A STAR WAS BORN!!

AN JOSE, CALIFORNIA -
ARCH 28, 2015
BUT THAT IS NOT WHERE THE STORY ENDS. I WAS BLESSED WITH THE HONOR OF POSTHUMOUSLY INDUCTING MY BROTHER, RANDY SAVAGE, INTO THE WWE HALL OF FAME.
I STAND BEFORE THE HALL OF FAME IN HONOR OF MY BROTHER WHO SEIZED EACH CARPE DIEM DAY WITH PASSION LIKE NO OTHER.
BORN RANDY MARIO POFFO HE BECAME THE MACHO MAN RANDY SAVAGE MADE IT COOL TO BE A WRESTLING FAN.
HIS MATCH WITH RICKY STEAMBOAT IN 1987 WAS ON A SCALE OF 1 TO 10 MUCH BETTER THAN 11.
HE SNAPPED INTO A SLIM JIM WITH HIS ICONIC VOICE HE EARNED A ROLE IN SPIDER-MAN WHICH MADE HIS FANS REJOICE.
WHEN THE MEGA POWERS EXPLODED THE STORYLINE WAS REAL LIFE'S TOO SHORT TO HOLD A GRUDGE IT'S TIME FOR US TO HEAL.
IN TRIUMPHANT JUBILATION WE CELEBRATE HIS NAME FINALLY THE MACHO MAN IS IN THE HALL OF FAME.
THE END.

Hulk Hogan

The Hulkster

Birth Name:	Terry Bollea
Born:	August 11, 1953 Augusta, Georgia
Height:	6' 7"
Weight:	302 lbs
Career:	1977-2015

A young Terry Bollea, the man who would become Hulk Hogan, began his career in entertainment as an amateur musician in Tampa, Florida, in the mid-1970's. While already working out vigorously in a local gym, he was actually beginning a career in finance at the time. During his training for that position at a bank, he had access to the financial statements of local wrestlers and their relatively prodigious incomes, prompting him to look into wrestling for himself.

Bollea eventually worked contacts in the Florida wrestling community until he wa connected with noted trainer, Hiro Matsuda, and granted a meeting in his gym, th ominously titled "Snake Pit". His training class famously included future rival Pau Orndorff and Killer Bee B. Brian Blair, and there is a timeless story of Matsud breaking Bollea's leg on the first day of training to "protect the business" of wrestlin and to prove a point to the aspiring wrestler that he was not ready to just walk int the ring.

He briefly wrestled for Championship Wrestling of Florida, including a match agains B. Brian Blair, and he worked for some time as a transferable masked wrestler calle The Super Destroyer. Becoming disenchanted with Matsuda's fierce training styl Bollea left wrestling for months, until Superstar Billy Graham connected him with promotion in Alabama, where he and Ed Leslie (later Brutus The Barber Beefcake teamed as The Boulder Brothers, efforts which soon earned them the attention o Jerry Jarrett and positions in Memphis' Continental Wrestling Association (CWA).

While in Memphis, Bollea appeared on a local talk show, coincidentally at the same time as actor and bodybuilder, Lou Ferrigno, who played The Incredible Hulk on television in the late 1970's. Bollea was notably larger than Ferrigno and was inspired by the size differential to use the Hulk moniker for himself, often billed as Terry "The Hulk" Boulder thereafter. He also sometimes went by the alias, Sterling Golden.

His first championship belt was the NWA Southeastern Heavyweight Championship, garnered in a win over Bob Roop in December, 1979, but lost a month later to Bob Armstrong. Bollea's first, brief run in the World Wrestling Federation (WWF) came in 1980, after Terry Funk introduced him to Vince McMahon, who suggested he use the ring name, Hogan.

Hogan spent 1981-83 in Verne Gagne's American Wrestling Association (AWA) while also working in New Japan Pro Wrestling (NJPW) for some periods. In the AWA, he feuded with the Heenans and Nick Bockwinkel before the WWF came calling again, as McMahon initiated his plans to expand to a nationwide promotion with Hogan as the centerpiece attraction.

On January 23, 1984, Hogan defeated The Iron Sheik at Madison Square Garden to win The WWF World Heavyweight Championship for the first time. From Gorilla Monsoon's announcement of Hulkamania's arrival after this match, the familiar, yet legendary, persona of Hulk Hogan quickly flourished, extending beyond the ring to larger pop culture. He previously appeared in the film, *Rocky III*, and, in 1985, teamed with friend and co-star, Mr. T, to take down Rowdy Roddy Piper and Mr. Wonderful Paul Orndorff at the inaugural Wrestlemania event.

Hogan's epic WWF run lasted a full decade, into 1993, before he moved on to World Championship Wrestling (WCW), winning the promotion's Heavyweight Championship over Ric Flair in his very first match, sparking a long-running feud. In a shocking heel turn, he was an inaugural member, along with Scott Hall and Kevin Nash, of the groundbreaking New World Order (nWo) stable at WCW, thereafter referring to himself as Hollywood Hogan. In 2005, he was inducted into the WWE Hall of Fame.

Jake Roberts

The Snake

Birth Name:	Aurelian Smith, Jr.
Born:	May 30, 1955 Gainesville, Texas
Height:	6' 6"
Weight:	249 lbs
Career:	1975-2015

The son of wrestler Grizzly Roberts and half-brother of fellow WWF Superstars, Sam Houston and Rockin' Robin, Jake the Snake Roberts began his own professional wrestling career in 1974 in Mid-South Wrestling and Georgia Championship Wrestling.

During an early 1980's match with The Grappler, Roberts executed an inverted headlock, tripped over his opponent's foot, fell backwards to the mat, and invented the DDT.

In 1984, Roberts joined Texas-based World Class Championship Wrestling (WCCW) and feuded with the Von Erichs, earning the Television Title belt and 6-Man Tag Team Title. He joined the World Wrestling Federation (WWF) in 1986 and soon began a timeless feud with Ricky "The Dragon" Steamboat that included an ongoing gimmick in which Roberts consistently brought a python and Steamboat a Komodo dragon to the ring. The python-in-a-bag bit was Roberts' staple throughout his career.

His superior mic skills earned him a talk segment, The Snake Pit, in 1986, and he continued to gain popularity despite the WWF's efforts to cast him as a true heel, resulting in short-lived feuds with The Macho Man Randy Savage and Hulk Hogan. Ultimately, Roberts made a full face turn and feuded with The Honky Tonk Man and later, Ravishing Rick Rude and even Andre the Giant and The Million Dollar Man Ted DiBiase. He spent a portion of 1992 in World Championship Wrestling (WCW) and continued to make appearances for many years before being inducted into the World Wrestling Entertainment (WWE) Hall of Fame in 2014.

Hacksaw Jim Duggan

The Developmental Years

Born:	January 14, 1954 Glens Falls, NY
Height:	6' 3"
Weight:	270 lbs
Career:	1979-Present

Young Jim Duggan spent his adolescence on ride-alongs with his father, a career Glens Falls police officer, and developing his athtletic skills. He excelled in football, basketball, track and field, and wrestling, achieving the New York State Championship in his senior year in high school. Several major college football programs, including Penn State and Ohio State heavily recruited Jim as an offensive lineman, but he ultimately selected Southern Methodist, given the opportunity to start immediately his first year.

Jim played four full seasons at Southern Methodist, earning All-Southwest Conference honors and serving as team captain. After graduation, the Atlanta Falcons of the National Football League (NFL) signed him to a free agent contract, but he suffered a season-ending injury in his first training camp. Upon his return to Southern Methodist for rehabilitation of his knee, he met fellow alumnus and owner of World Class Championship Wrestling, Fritz Von Erich, who encouraged him to consider joining the ranks of professional wrestlers at his Texas-based promotion.

Steadfast in his desire to continue his football career, Jim turned down Von Erich's offer and signed with the Toronto Argonauts of the Canadian Football League (CFL) but lasted only two games before being released. In 1979, he reported to the legendary Sportatorium in Dallas to try out for Big-Time Wrestling with Gary Hart, showing enough promise in a series of drills and holds to begin training with David Manning, eventually leading to his debut, as Big Jim Duggan, in a tag team with Gorgeous Gino Hernandez, when Hernandez' billed partner was a late arrival to the event.

writer **John E. Crowther**
@crowman1971

artist **Rich Perotta**
@RichPerottaArt

colorist **Vito Potenza**
@PiwiTFP

letterer **Jayson Kretzer**
@JaysonKretzer

editor/designer **Kevin LaPorte**
@kevinlaporte

88. COPPS COLISEUM.
MILTON, ONTARIO, CANADA
THAT'S HACKSAW JIM DUGGAN!!
HOOOOOOO!!!
THE YEAR WAS 1988, THE FIRST EVER WORLD WRESTLING FEDERATION ROYAL RUMBLE AND, TO THE ROAR OF THE THOUSANDS IN ATTENDANCE I WAS MARCHING TO THE RING, THE THIRTEENTH ENTRANT IN THE FIRST EVER ROYAL RUMBLE MATCH.
JIM DUGGAN HAD RETURNED TO HAMILTON (BUT WE'LL DISCUSS THAT LATER).

I WAS MET RINGSIDE BY THE LEGENDARY KING HARLEY RACE.
WHAP!
A QUICK FOREARM SENT THE KING BACK TO THE SHOWERS.
I GLANCED UP AT THE RING, SOAKING IN THE MELEE THAT WAS THE ROYAL RUMBLE. TWENTY COMPETITORS, BEGINNING WITH TWO, AND ADDING AN ADDITIONAL OPPONENT EVERY TWO MINUTES.
A NO-HOLDS-BARRED BRAWL...WHEREIN EACH MAN IS ELIMINATED BY BEING TOSSED OVER THE TOP ROPE. A MATCH DESIGNED FOR THE HACKSAW.
BATTLING IN THE RING WERE SOME OF THE TOUGHEST MEN IN THE BUSINESS...JUMPING JIM BRUNZELL, NIKOLAI VOLKOFF, BRET "THE HITMAN" HART, JIM "THE ANVIL" NEIDHART, DON MURACO, DANGEROUS DANNY DAVIS, SAM HOUSTON, AND JAKE "THE SNAKE" ROBERTS.
NO SWEAT.

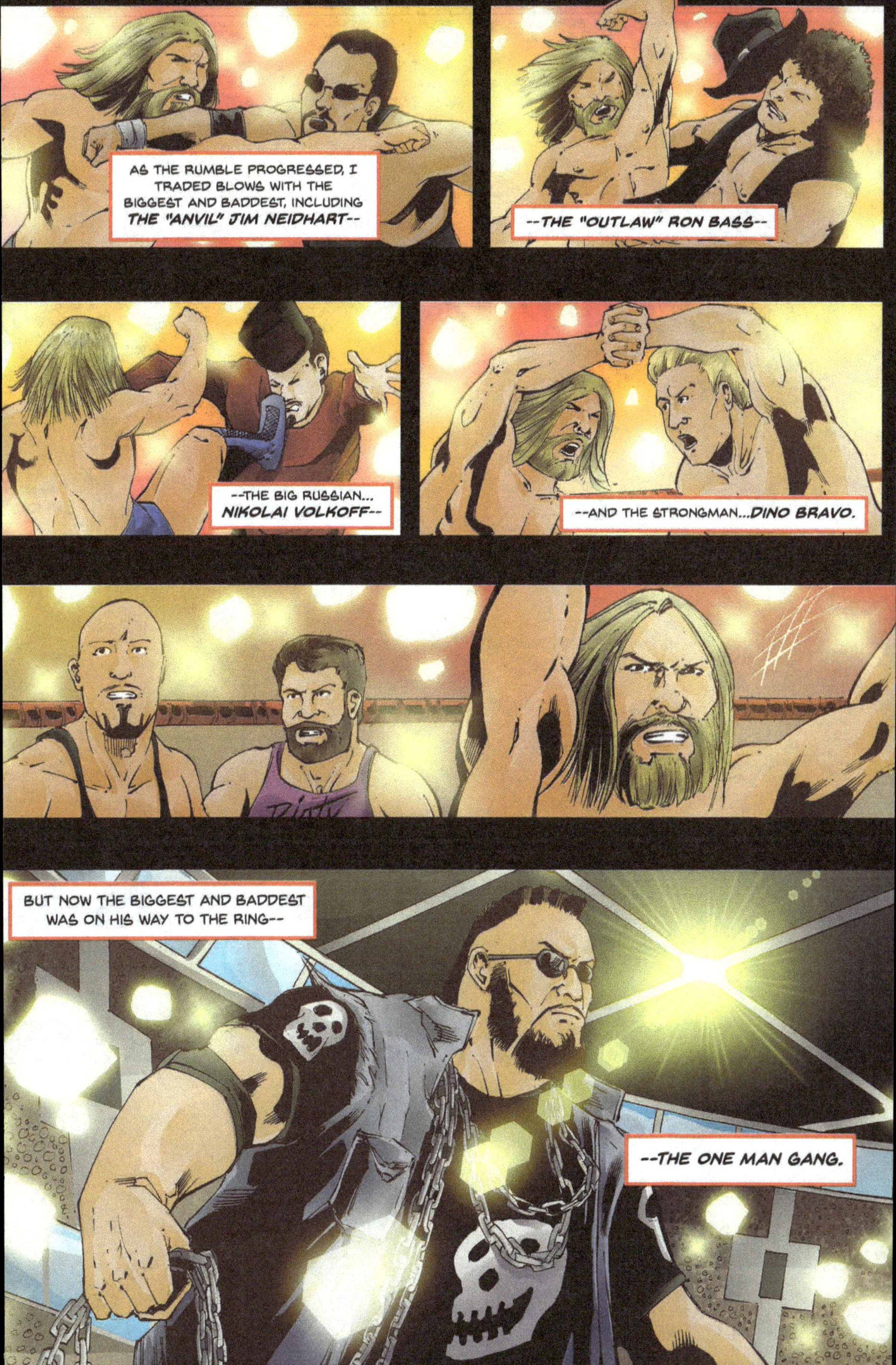

AS THE RUMBLE PROGRESSED, I TRADED BLOWS WITH THE BIGGEST AND BADDEST, INCLUDING ***THE "ANVIL" JIM NEIDHART--***

--***THE "OUTLAW"*** RON BASS--

WHEN GANG ENTERED THE RING AT NUMBER 19, THE MATCH INTENSIFIED AND THE ELIMINATIONS INCREASED, WITH GANG ELIMINATING BRIAN BLAIR....
...AND JAKE "THE SNAKE" ROBERTS.
AND ME ELIMINATING VOLKOFF--
U.S.S.R.
--AND DELIVERING MY SIGNATURE SHOULDER BLOCK TO DANNY DAVIS--
...SENDING HIM OVER THE TOP ROPE AND BACK TO THE LOCKER ROOM.

WE WERE DOWN TO FOUR: ME, ONE MAN GANG, DON MURACO, AND DINO BRAVO. EVERY MAN FOR HIMSELF.
BRAVO AND GANG PAIRED AGAINST DON MURACO--
ELIMINATING THE ROCK WITH A BULL RUSH FROM GANG--
--BEFORE SETTING THEIR SIGHTS ON ME.

I WENT TOE-TO-TOE WITH BOTH MEN. A PIER 6 BRAWL.
THE MATCH HAD TAKEN A TOLL ON ME PHYSICALLY AND THESE TWO GIANTS CLEARLY HAD THE ADVANTAGE.
THEY SET ME UP FOR ELIMINATION--
--BUT THEY MISCALCULATED, AND BRAVO WAS OUT--
--LEAVING JUST ME AND THE GANG.

GANG GLARED AT ME WITH THOSE HUNGRY EYES.
AND CHARGED.
FOR A BIG MAN, HE WAS QUICK. BUT I WAS *QUICKER*.
HOOOOOOO!!!
I WAS THE LONE MAN LEFT IN THE RING. THE *FIRST WINNER* OF THE ROYAL RUMBLE. A FUTURE *WWE HALL OF FAMER*. AND IN THE LAST PLACE IN THE WORLD I THOUGHT I'D BE.

I WAS BORN JAMES EDWARD DUGGAN, JR., ON JANUARY 14, 1954, IN THE TOWN OF GLENS FALLS, NEW YORK.
I ENTERED THE WORLD SERENADING MY FOLKS WITH MY RECOGNIZABLE--
HOOOOOOOOOOO
BEING THE YOUNGEST IN A HOUSEHOLD WITH THREE OLDER SISTERS, I HAD TO BE SLY TO GET MY WAY--
--FAST TO GET MY HEARTY PORTION OF DINNER, AND ROUGH TO EARN RESPECT--

--BUT IT WAS THE INFLUENCE OF MY FATHER, NIGHT CAPTAIN AND FUTURE CHIEF OF POLICE FOR GLENS FALLS, THAT WAS THE MAJOR MOTIVATING FACTOR IN MY FORMATIVE YEARS.
CAR 7--WE HAVE A CODE 1...10-51...AT THE CORNER OF GLEN AND WARREN STREETS. PLEASE PROCEED.
SOUNDS LIKE SOMEONE'S DRANK THEIR WAY INTO A PUDDLE, CAP'N.
TIME TO GO *FISHIN'!*
READY FOR A *LIL' FUN,* SON?
SURE, DAD!

HEY, BUD...YOU AWAKE?
MEH... ECK UM... MEH BEH.
COME ON, BUDDY. I THINK YOU COULD USE A LIL' DETOX IN THE CLINK.
MEH MUMMA... ESH WID MEH DIG... TEK ME BEH...
YEAH...YEAH. GET IN THERE, TOUGH GUY!
NEEDLESS TO SAY, NIGHTS ON PATROL WITH MY FATHER STRENGTHENED MY CHARACTER, BUILDING ME INTO THE 'TOUGH GUY' I WOULD LATER BECOME.
ZZZZz...

ST. MARY'S ACADEMY IS A PRIVATE CATHOLIC SCHOOL IN GLENS FALLS.
IT'S WHERE I STUDIED--
--AND WHERE I HONED MY ATHLETIC SKILLS FROM GRADE SCHOOL UNTIL JUNIOR HIGH.

I GREW QUICKLY AS AN ATHLETE--
--AND OTHERS BEGAN TO TAKE NOTICE, INCLUDING MY FELLOW STUDENTS--
--AND *MY FATHER.*
I THINK YOU SHOULD TRANSFER, SON. DON'T GET ME WRONG, ST. MARY'S IS A GREAT SCHOOL.
BUT YOU'VE GOT A *GOD-GIVEN GIFT* WITH FOOTBALL AND GLENS FALLS HIGH IS YOUR TICKET TO GETTING NOTICED.
IT WAS DECIDED...I WOULD TRANSFER TO MY CROSS-TOWN RIVAL, GLENS FALLS HIGH SCHOOL. THE FIRST DUGGAN KID NOT TO GRADUATE FROM ST. MARY'S. I WAS ABOUT TO SUIT UP AS A *GLENS FALLS INDIAN!*

COMING FROM ST. MARY'S TO THE PUBLIC SCHOOL WAS A CHANGE.
I WAS USED TO WEARING JACKETS AND TIES AS OPPOSED TO BLUE JEANS AND T-SHIRTS, BUT I ADJUSTED QUICKLY--
--EARNING 10 VARSITY LETTERS, AS I CONTINUED MY ATHLIETC DOMINANCE ON THE FOOTBALL FIELD--
-THE BASKETBALL COURT--
--AT TRACK AND FIELD, WHERE I SET THE SCHOOL RECORED IN THE SHOT PUT (WHICH STILL STANDS TODAY).

--AND WRESTLING WHERE MY COACH, BOB CARY--
COACH
--HELPED GUIDE ME TO AN UNDEFEATED SEASON--
--AND A 1-POINT VICTORY OVER MY FINAL OPPONENT (A FUTURE QUALIFIER FOR THE 1980 SUMMER OPYMPICS) FOR THE NEW YORK STATE CHAMPIONSHIP MY SENIOR YEAR.

BUT FOOTBALL WAS MY SPORT.
DEFENDING THE QUARTERBACK WAS MY SPECIALTY.
AND I WAS GOOD AT IT.

GOOD ENOUGH TO CATCH THE ATTENTION OF SUCH COACHING GREATS AS FRAN CURCI, FROM THE UNIVERSITY OF KENTUCKY AND FLOYD "BEN" SCHWARTZWALDER FROM SYRACUSE UNIVERSITY--
. . .AND THE GREAT JOE PATERNO FROM PENN STATE.
BUT OHIO STATE LEGEND WOODY HAYES HAD ME SOLD--
--I WOULD BE AN OHIO STATE BUCKEYE!

BUT THE COACHES FROM **SOUTHERN METHODIST UNIVERSITY** WERE SMART. THEY MET MY MOM.
MOM! I'VE DECIDED. I'M GOING TO **OHIO STATE!** I'M GONNA BE A--
SLOW DOWN, HONEY.
JIM, THIS IS **COACH CUTBIRTH** FROM SOUTHWEST METHODIST. HE'S COME ALL THE WAY FROM DALLAS, TEXAS TO SEE YOU.
GREAT TO MEET YOU, JIM. LET'S HAVE A SEAT.
JIM, I UNDERSTAND THE EXCITEMENT OF PLAYING AT OHIO STATE UNDER **COACH HAYES**. THE MAN'S A LEGEND. BUT WE CAN GIVE YOU SOMETHING HE CAN'T.
WHAT'S THAT, SIR?
OHIO STATE CAN PUT YOU ON THE ROSTER, BUT **SMU** CAN PUT YOU ON THE FIELD. FOUR YEARS AS A STARTER AND A STRONG SHOT AT THE NATIONAL FOOTBALL LEAGUE. WHADDA YOU SAY?

SO, WITH A GREAT SALES PITCH FROM COACH CUTBIRTH, SOME GENTLE PRODDING BY MY MOTHER, AND THE ENCOURAGEMENT OF MY HIGH SCHOOL COACH PUTT LAMAY--
--I BECAME A *MUSTANG*.
I WAS ON MY WAY TO DALLAS, TEXAS, AND SOUTHERN METHODIST UNIVERSITY.

I HIT THE SMU CAMPUS AND JUMPED RIGHT INTO THE FRAY.
QUICKLY BECOMING A DOMINATING FORCE ON THE PRACTICE FIELD--
--AND PANCAKING A FEW DEFENDERS ALONG THE WAY.
YOU AIN'T TOUCHIN' MY QUARTERBACK, TOUGH GUY.
UMPHH!

COME ON GUYS! WHERE'S YOU
BLOCKING!?
DUGGAN, GET IN THERE!!

ONCE I ENTERED THE GAME THAT DAY, I *NEVER LOOKED BACK*--
--SETTING THE SMU RECORD FOR CONSECUTIVE STARTS--
--STARTING FROM THE THIRD GAME OF MY FRESHMAN YEAR, TO THE FINAL GAME OF MY SENIOR SEASON--
--SERVING AS TEAM CAPTAIN THAT LAST CAMPAIGN--
--AND EARNING *ALL SOUTHWEST CONFERENCE HONORS.*

FOLLOWING MY SENIOR SEASON AT SMU, I WENT UNDRAFTED BY THE NATIONAL FOOTBALL LEAGUE.
FURMAN UNIVERSITY
BEING A DUGGAN, I WOULDN'T LET THAT STOP ME. I HEADED TO **FURMAN UNIVERSITY** IN GREENVILLE, SOUTH CAROLINA--
--FOR A TRYOUT WITH THE **ATLANTA FALCONS.**
NFL TRAINING CAMP WAS DIFFICULT--
--ONE OF THE MOST DIFFICULT EXPERIENCES I HAVE EVER HAD TO ENDURE.
BUT I DID ENDURE--
--AND SIGNED A FREE AGENT CONTRACT WITH THE FALCONS--

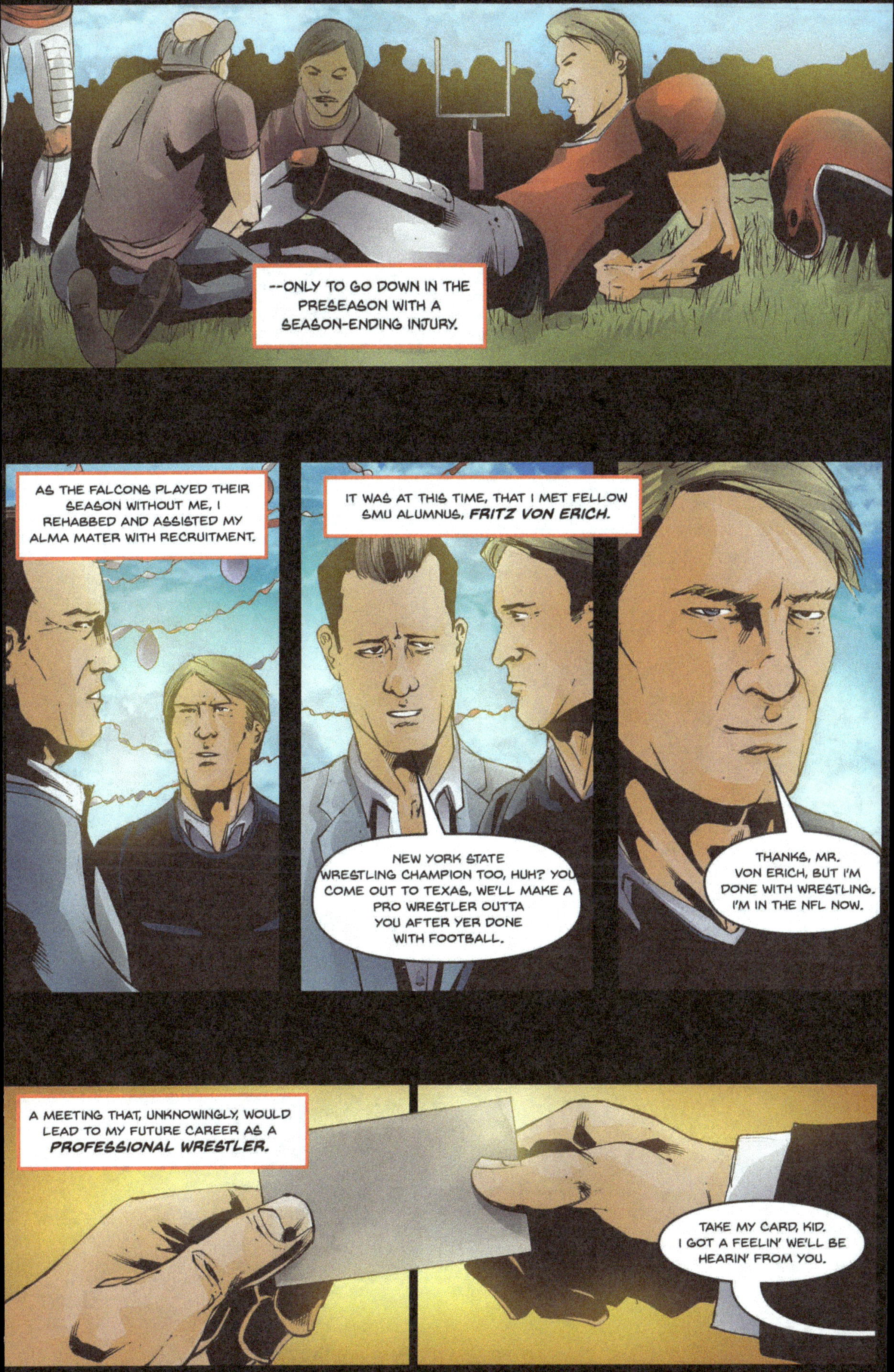

--ONLY TO GO DOWN IN THE PRESEASON WITH A SEASON-ENDING INJURY.

AS THE FALCONS PLAYED THEIR SEASON WITHOUT ME, I REHABBED AND ASSISTED MY ALMA MATER WITH RECRUITMENT.

IT WAS AT THIS TIME, THAT I MET FELLOW SMU ALUMNUS, ***FRITZ VON ERICH.***

NEW YORK STATE WRESTLING CHAMPION TOO, HUH? YOU COME OUT TO TEXAS, WE'LL MAKE A PRO WRESTLER OUTTA YOU AFTER YER DONE WITH FOOTBALL.

THANKS, MR. VON ERICH, BUT I'M DONE WITH WRESTLING. I'M IN THE NFL NOW.

I RETURNED TO THE FALCONS AFTER A YEAR OF REHABILITATION, ONLY TO BE RELEASED BY THE TEAM.
BUT FOOTBALL WAS MY DREAM, AND I WAS *PERSISTENT*.
TORONTO, ONTARIO, CANADA AND THE *CANADIAN FOOTBALL LEAGUE* WERE MY NEXT DESTINATIONS.
60

I MADE THE TEAM AND PLAYED WELL--
HARPER
88
YOU KNOW HOW IT IS, JIM. IT'S A NUMBERS GAME. WE'VE GOT TO LET YOU GO.
--BUT IT WAS NOT MEANT TO BE.
FOLLOWING THE SECOND GAME OF THE SEASON IN HAMILTON, ONTARIO, CANADA, I WAS LET GO.
MY DREAM OF PROFESSIONAL FOOTBALL HAD COME TO A CLOSE--
Fritz Von Erich
Professional Wrestling
Dallas, Texas
555-042-2014

B. Brian Blair

The Developmental Years

Born: January 12, 1959
Gary, Indiana
Spouses: Mike McGuirk
Toni Sabella
Height: 6' 1"
Weight: 235 lbs
Career: 1977-2019

B. Brian Blair grew up in the nation's capitol of professional wrestling, Tampa, Florida. He decided early in life that he would become a pro wrestler, and he began physical training as an adolescent, earning letters in football, baseball, track and field, and wrestling, culminating in a football scholarship from the University of Louisville.

In 1975, he started training with the legendary Hiro Matsuda to learn the art of pro wrestling.

Art by Nathan Smith

Few of those who trained with Matsuda made it through the exclusive program, and Blair's surviving class included such future superstars as Hulk Hogan and Mr. Wonderful Paul Orndorff. After two years of training, he made his in-ring debut for Eddie Graham's Championship Wrestling of Florida as part of a tag team with Skip Young in a match against Ivan Koloff and Pat Patterson. His first title came in the National Wrestling Alliance (NWA) Central States promotion, where he and "Bulldog" Bob Brown teamed to take the Tag Team Championship. The Junior Heavyweight Championship with an NWA promotion in Oklahoma soon followed in 1978.

These and other tag team successes in NWA territories ultimately led to a brief stint in the World Wrestling Federation (WWF) in 1980, followed by a run as NWA American Tag Team Champion alongside Al Madril and a NWA Florida Championship singles win over Jimmy Garvin and a Southern Heavyweight Championship claimed from Ravishing Rick Rude. Upon Blair's return to the WWF, Hulk Hogan himself recommended he team with new WWF signee, Jumpin' Jim Brunzell.

Jumpin' Jim Brunzell

The Developmental Years

Born:	August 13, 1949 Kansas City, Missouri
Spouse:	Mary Iten
Height:	5' 10"
Weight:	235 lbs
Career:	1972-1999

James Brunzell was a three-sport athlete during high school in White Bear Lake, Minnesota before starting as a tight end for the University of Minnesota Golden Gophers in 1969. It was during this time that he met quarterback Greg Gagne, son of wrestling legend, Verne Gagne. After an attempt at a career in pro football and upon returning to Minnesota, Brunzell reconnected with Gagne, who urged him to train as a professional wrestler.

In 1972, he joined the training arm of Verne Gagne's American Wrestling Alliance (AWA), learning the ropes from Billy Robinson alongside Greg Gagne, Ken Patera, and Ric Flair. After initial in-ring work, the AWA sent Brunzell to perform in NWA Central States, where he teamed with Mike George to win the promotion's Tag Team Championship in 1973. While working Central States, he had opportunity to learn from Harley Race and Jack Brisco before a brief span working in Japan in 1974.

The accumulated experience culminated in a return to the AWA in 1975 to team with old friend, Greg Gagne, as The High Flyers. The pair became fast fan favorites and ultimately captured the AWA World Tag Team Championship in 1977, besting the previous belt holders, Blackjack Lanza and Bobby Duncum, only to soon forfeit the titles due to a non-wrestling injury to Brunzell. The team enjoyed a second AWA Championship run in the early 1980's before Brunzell moved on to the WWF with the recommendation of Hulk Hogan, who went on to introduce him to his next great tag team partner, B. Brian Blair, with whom he would form The Killer Bees.

the KILLER BEES

B. BRIAN BLAIR

writer John E. Crowther
@crowman1971

artist Dell Barras
@DellBarras

colorist Andrew Pate
@Andrew_Pate

letterer Jayson Kretzer
@JaysonKretzer

editor/designer Kevin LaPorte
@kevinlaporte

GARY, INDIANA, 1968
WHILE A YOUNG ACTIVE BOY IN GARY, INDIANA, THE LOCAL PREACHER ONCE TOLD ME I COULD BE ANYTHING I WANTED TO BE WHEN I GREW UP...I JUST NEEDED TO PRAY.
I NARROWED IT DOWN TO TWO CHOICES... MILLIONAIRE OR I COULD HELP PEOPLE AND BE A SUPERHERO.
I PICKED SUPERHERO, BECAUSE I WANTED TO FLY...
IT DIDN'T TAKE ME LONG TO REALIZE THAT SUPERHEROES COULDN'T FLY.... BUT PROFESSIONAL WRESTLERS? THEY COULD SOAR.

SO...PROFESSIONAL WRESTLER IT WOULD BE. A REAL LIFE SUPERHERO.
BUT IF I TRULY WANTED TO ACHIEVE MY GOAL, IT WOULD TAKE MORE THAN PRAYER SO, AT AN EARLY AGE, I BEGAN TO TRAIN.
THEN WORD CAME. WE WERE RELOCATING TO TAMPA, FLORIDA FOR MY FATHER'S WORK. TAMPA... THE HOTBED OF PROFESSIONAL WRESTLING.

TAMPA, FLORIDA
TAMPA BAY TECH HIGH SCHOOL
ONCE IN TAMPA, FLORIDA, I CONTINUED TO TRAIN. EVENTUALLY BECOMING A 4-SPORT STAR FOR THE TAMPA BAY TECH TITANS, EARNING LETTERS IN FOOTBALL, BASEBALL, TRACK & FIELD, AND WRESTLING.

I WAS RECOGNIZED AND AWARDED THE HIGHEST ACCOLADES FOR MY HIGH SCHOOL ATHLETIC ACHIEVEMENTS--
TITAN PRIDE
T
TAMPA BAY TECH
--INCLUDING AN ATHLETIC SCHOLARSHIP TO PLAY FOOTBALL AT THE UNIVERSITY OF LOUISVILLE--
WRESTLIN
PRO WRESTLING
--BUT PROFESSIONAL WRESTLING REMAINED MY DREAM.
RING

FORT HOMER W. HESTERLY ARMORY, TAMPA, FLORIDA.
CHAMPIONSHIP WRESTLING FROM FLORIDA TONIGHT!
AS A TEENAGER, I WOULD SPEND COUNTLESS HOURS ATTENDING WRESTLING MATCHES AT THE FORT HOWARD HESTERLY ARMORY, MORE POPULARLY KNOWN AS "THE ARMORY"; HOME TO EDDIE GRAHAM'S CHAMPIONSHIP WRESTLING FROM FLORIDA.
ON GOOD NIGHTS, I WOULD SOMETIMES CHANCE UPON A FREE TICKET TO THE SHOW...
HERE YOU GO KID! HAVE FUN. THERE ARE SOME GREAT MATCHES TONIGHT.
THANKS!!
MR. KEIRN! CAN I HELP YOU WITH YOUR BAG?
AND ON OTHER NIGHTS, IF I WAS LUCKY, I WOULD ASSIST WRESTLERS SUCH AS STEVE KEIRN WITH THEIR EQUIPMENT--
SURE BRIAN! HEADS UP!
--GAINING MYSELF ACCESS TO THE LOCKER ROOM AND THE MATCHES.
HEY BRIAN!
HEY KID, ENJOY THE SHOW!

THE LIGHTS, THE CHARACTERS, THE CROWDS, AND THE *INTENSITY*--
I SOAKED IN THE MATCHES OF SUCH GREATS AS *DUSTY RHODES*--
THIS WAS A WORLD I WANTED TO BE A PART OF.
FORMER TRAINERS, *BUDDY COLT*--

JACK BRISCO--
WHAM!
AND PEERS, SUCH AS DON MURACO.
KAPOW!!

1975

BECOMING A PROFESSIONAL WRESTLER WOULD REQUIRE MORE THAN PLAYING HIGH SCHOOL SPORTS AND ATTENDING MATCHES.

GYM

IT REQUIRED REAL TRAINING. SO I SOUGHT OUT THE BEST--

HIRO MATSUDA.

TRAINING WITH MATSUDA WAS STRENUOUS, BUT REWARDING.
EACH DAY WOULD BEGIN WITH FIVE SETS OF 100 SQUATS AND FIVE SETS OF 100 PUSH-UPS, *BEFORE* STEPPING INTO THE RING.
ALL THIS, WITHOUT AIR CONDITIONING, IN THE SWELTERING FLORIDA HEAT.

MATSUDA TRAINED US IN A JIU JITSU STYLE OF PROFESSIONAL WRESTLING--
BELIEVING THAT NOT ONLY MUST WRESTLERS BE ABLE TO PERFORM IN THE RING--
WRESTLERS MUST ALSO BE ABLE TO DEFEND THEMSELVES FROM UNRULY FANS.
WHAMM

THE INTENSE TRAINING WAS TAXING ON THE WRESTLERS BOTH MENTALLY AND PHYSICALLY.
ARRGH!
WHAT'S A MATTER, BRIAN? YOU NO PUKE TODAY.
THAT'S BECAUSE I HAVEN'T EATEN SINCE THE LAST TIME I ATE.
THAT'S MY BOY!!

A MAJORITY OF WRESTLERS WHO TRAINED WITH MATSUDA DIDN'T MAKE THE CUT AND WALKED AWAY.
GYM
OF THE 100 OR SO MEN I TRAINED WITH, A SELECT FEW GRADUATED...MYSELF, HULK HOGAN, AND PAUL ORNDORFF INCLUDED.
IN 1977, AFTER TWO YEARS OF TRAINING WITH MATSUDA, I WAS READY TO MAKE MY RING DEBUT--
WITH EDDIE GRAHAM'S CHAMPIONSHIP WRESTLING FROM FLORIDA, IN A TAG TEAM MATCH WITH SKIP YOUNG AGAINST OUR OPPONENTS..."THE RUSSIAN BEAR" IVAN KOLOFF AND PAT PATTERSON.

FIRST OFFICIAL MATCH, BRIAN. GO GET 'EM!
THANKS DON.
....AND THEIR OPPONENTS--
FROM TAMPA, FLORIDA--
SKIP YOUNG AND BRIAN
BLAIRRRRRR!!
...AND YOUR WINNERS...BY PIN FALL--
--THE TEAM OF PAT PATTERSON AND "THE RUSSIAN BEAR... IVAN KOLOFF!!

KANSAS CITY, MISSOURI, 1978
AFTER MY START IN FLORIDA, I TRAVELED TO KANSAS CITY, MISSOURI, TO WRESTLE FOR THE NWA -- CENTRAL STATES PROMOTION.
CENTRAL STATES NWA PROFESSIONAL WRESTLING - TONIGHT.
TICKETS
IT WAS IN KANSAS CITY THAT I WAS TEAMED WITH "BULLDOG" BOB BROWN--

...WITH WHOM I WOULD BEGIN MY FIRST TITLE REIGN AS THE CENTRAL STATES TAG TEAM CHAMPIONS.
YOUR WINNERS... AND NEW CENTRAL STATES TAG TEAM CHAMPIONS--
BRIAN BLAIR AND THE "BULLDOG" BOB BROWNNNN!

ALSO AT THIS TIME, I WAS MAKING APPEARANCES FOR THE NWA TRI-STATE PROMOTION OF LEROY MCGUIRK AND AURELIAN "GRIZZLY" SMITH--
ARKANSAS
OKLAHOM
LOUISIANA
--WHICH ENCOMPASSED THE STATES OF ARKANSAS, OKLAHOMA, AND LOUISIANA.
KRACK!
I WAS QUICKLY BECOMING A FAN FAVORITE IN THE TRI-STATE PROMOTION...

...AND IT WAS HERE, IN OKLAHOMA, THAT, ALBEIT SHORT, I WON AND HAD MY FIRST SINGLES CHAMPIONSHIP TITLE REIGN.
....THE CHALLENGER ...FROM TAMPA, FLORIDA--
BRIAN BLAIRRRRRR!!
YOUR WINNER...AND NEW JUNIOR HEAVYWEIGHT CHAMPION--
BRIAN BLAIRRR!!!

IN 1980, THROUGH VINCE MCMAHON, SR., I HAD MY FIRST STINT WITH THE WWF
TOURING WITH THE ORGANIZATION IN JAPAN AND WRESTLING NEW JAPAN PRO WRESTLING ICONS--
NIPPON
ANTONIO INOKI AND--
--TATSUMI FUJINAMI.

FOLLOWING MY TOUR OF JAPAN WITH THE WWF, I RETURNED TO THE UNITED STATES, WHERE I TEAMED WITH AL MADRIL TO WIN THE NWA AMERICAN TAG TEAM CHAMPIONSHIP--
TEXAS
ARRIVALS
--A TITLE WE DEFENDED SUCCESSFULLY FOR THREE MONTHS.
BLAIR AND MADRIL
WRESTLING CHAMPIONS

WHICH, IN TURN, WAS FOLLOWED BY A RETURN TO MY WRESTLING ROOTS--
FLORIDA CHAMPIONSHIP WRESTLING, WHERE I FIRST DEFEATED JIMMY GARVIN FOR THE NWA FLORIDA CHAMPIONSHIP...
STATE OF FLORIDA

....AND LATER "RAVISHING" RICK RUDE, FOR THE--
--SOUTHERN HEAVYWEIGHT CHAMPIONSHIP.

FOLLOWING MY CHAMPIONSHIP RUN IN FLORIDA, I RETURNED TO THE WWE, WHERE I PARTNERED WITH TONY GAREA.
WE WERE A SUCCESSFUL TEAM, WINNING MOST OF OUR MATCHES....BUT I WAS LOOKING FOR A SPECIAL POP--
--THE HOOK THAT WOULD TRULY PUT ME OVER WITH THE FANS.

THAT WAS WHEN I WAS APPROACHED BY MY FRIEND AND FELLOW TRAINEE WITH HIRO MATSUDA, HULK HOGAN.
THERE'S SOMEONE I WANT YOU TO MEET. I THINK THE TWO OF YOU WOULD MAKE A FANTASTIC TAG TEAM.
WHO'S THAT, TERRY?
"HIS NAME'S JIM BRUNZELL. BEST DROPKICK IN WRESTLING, BROTHER."
RUNZELL....ONE-HALF OF THE AWA ORLD TAG TEAM CHAMPION HIGH LYERS, WITH GREG GAGNE?"
I'VE READ ABOUT HIM. HE'S A GREAT WRESTLER AND THE FANS LOVE HIM.
AND HE JUST SIGNED WITH THE WWF. HE'S GOING TO BE IN BRANTFORD. LET ME INTRODUCE THE TWO OF YOU.

BRANTFORD, ONTARIO, CANADA, 1985
IT WAS IN BRANTFORD, ONTARIO, CANADA, THAT I WAS INTRODUCED TO JIM BRUNZELL WHO WOULD BECOME MY TAG TEAM PARTNER.
I LIKE THE PAIRING, BOYS.
THE TEAM WAS FORMED, BUT WE NEEDED AN ANGLE. WE NEEDED A NAME. THAT TASK WAS PUT TO US THAT DAY BY LEGENDARY CANADIAN WRESTLER AND A CREATOR OF WRESTLEMANIA, GEORGE SCOTT.
VINCE WANTS A TEAM WITH A CATCHY NAME--
--THINK OF SOMETHING.

the KILLER BEES

JUMPIN' JIM BRUNZELL

writer John E. Crowther
@crowman1971

artist Dell Barras
@DellBarras

colorist Andrew Pate
@Andrew_Pate

editor/designer Kevin LaPorte
@kevinlaporte

WINNIPEG, MANITOBA, CANADA. JULY 16, 1981
I'M ABOUT TO MARCH TO THE RING FOR ONE OF THE BIGGEST MATCHES OF MY CAREER.
KNOCK 'EM DEAD, JIMMY!
I'M ABOUT TO TAKE THE RING FOR WHAT WOULD BE THE MOST MEMORABLE SINGLES MATCH OF MY CAREER.
I WAS ABOUT TO CHALLENGE NICK BOCKWINKEL FOR THE AWA WORLD HEAVYWEIGHT CHAMPIONSHIP.

BOCKWINKEL, WHO WOULD BECOME A FOUR-TIME AWA WORLD HEAVY-WEIGHT CHAMPION AND WWE HALL OF FAMER, AND I WERE ABOUT TO HAVE THE MATCH OF A LIFETIME.

AT THE TIME, I WAS A TWO-TIME AWA WORLD TAG TEAM CHAMPION AS A MEMBER OF THE HIGH FLYERS WITH GREG GAGNE...AND A FAN FAVORITE.

I DECIDED TO GO AT THE CHAMPION EARLY...

...TAKE HIM OUT OF HIS GAME.

BUT BOCKWINKEL WOULDN'T GIVE UP EASILY. HE HAD RECENTLY REGAINED THE TITLE FROM A RETIRED VERNE GAGNE, FOLLOWING A PRIOR REIGN OF NEARLY FIVE YEARS.
THIRTY MINUTES INTO THE MATCH, AND I HAD A WAR ON MY HANDS.
HE LOCKED IN HIS SIGNATURE SLEEPER HOLD. I HAD TO BREAK FREE, OR IT WAS LIGHTS OUT.
OUT OF DESPERATION, I DROVE HIM INTO THE TURNBUCKLE, BREAKING THE HOLD.
THE CHAMPION WAS STUNNED WITH ONE MINUTE REMAINING.

FTER TWO QUICK STRIKES WITH MY CELEBRATED
ROP KICK, THE HIGHEST IN THE INDUSTRY, I HAD
HE CHAMPION LOCKED IN THE FIGURE-FOUR.
OCKWINKEL WAS READY TO SURRENDER. I WOULD
E THE NEW AWA WORLD HEAVYWEIGHT...
DING DING DING
LADIES AND GENTLEMEN, AFTER ONE HOUR, I DECLARE A DRAW BETWEEN THE CHALLENGER, JIM BRUNZELL, AND THE CHAMPION, NICK BOCKWINKEL!
WHILE I DIDN'T WIN THE CHAMPIONSHIP THAT NIGHT IN CANADA, I WAS AT THE TOP OF MY GAME, HAVING WRESTLED IN THE GREATEST MATCH OF MY CAREER...BUT I'VE GOTTEN AHEAD OF MYSELF.

I WAS BORN JAMES BRUNZELL, ON AUGUST 13, 1949, IN KANSAS CITY, MISSOURI, THE SON OF A NAVY PILOT. YOU COULD SAY I WAS BORN TO FLY.
I ATTENDED HIGH SCHOOL IN WHITE BEAR LAKE, MINNESOTA, WHERE I WAS A 3-SPORT ATHLETE, COMPETING IN BASKETBALL...
...LEADING THE FOOTBALL TEAM IN RECEIVING AND SCORING...
...AND WINNING THE 1967 MINNESOTA INDOOR AND OUTDOOR STATE CHAMPIONSHIPS IN THE HIGH JUMP. I WAS DEFINITELY BORN TO FLY.

FOLLOWING MY GRADUATION FROM HIGH SCHOOL, I ATTENDED THE UNIVERSITY OF MINNESOTA...

IVERSITY OF MINNESOTA •

...WHERE I WAS A WALK-ON PLAYER FOR THE GOLDEN GOPHERS...

...UNDER LEGENDARY HEAD FOOTBALL COACH, ***MURRAY WARMATH...***

...EVENTUALLY STARTING AS A SPLIT-END BY MY JUNIOR YEAR IN 1969.

WHEN MY FOOTBALL ELIGIBILITY AT THE UNIVERSITY OF MINNESOTA EXPIRED, I PLAYED A YEAR OF SEMI-PROFESSIONAL FOOTBALL, BEFORE SIGNING A FREE AGENT CONTACT IN 1971 WITH THE WASHINGTON REDSKINS OF THE NATIONAL FOOTBALL LEAGUE AND PARTICIPATING IN A TRYOUT AT GEORGE WASHINGTON UNIVERSITY.
TALACT
MY FREE AGENT TRYOUT WAS RIGOROUS, BUT I WAS DETERMINED, HAVING RUN A 4.65 IN THE 40-YARD DASH IN COLLEGE.
I OUTRAN ALL COMPETING TIGHT ENDS AT THE TRYOUT WITH A 4.9 IN THE 40 ON A THICK MUDDY FIELD.
ALAS, WHILE MY NUMBERS WERE IMPRESSIVE, I WAS NOT ASKED BACK BY THE REDSKINS, AND MY SHORT-LIVED PROFESSIONAL FOOTBALL CAREER WAS OVER.
BUT, AS EVERY ENDING IS A NEW BEGINNING, I RE-ENROLLED AT THE UNIVERSITY OF MINNESOTA TO COMPLETE MY COLLEGE EDUCATION.

SHORTLY AFTER MY RETURN TO THE UNIVERSITY, I RECONNECTED WITH MY FORMER FOOTBALL TEAMMATE, GREG GAGNE. GREG HAD BEEN A QUARTERBACK FOR THE GOLDEN GOPHERS MY FRESHMAN YEAR, BUT HAD TRANSFERRED TO THE UNIVERSITY OF WYOMING.
SURE, GREG. WHAT TIME? SEE YOU THERE.
AS I WAS SAYING, YOU KNOW MY DAD, VERNE? YOU KNOW HE OWNS THE AMERICAN WRESTLING ALLIANCE?
SURE, I DO. WHAT'RE YOU GETTING AT?
THEY'RE ALWAYS SCOUTING FOR NEW TALENT, AND I'VE GOTTA BE HONEST WITH YOU, JIM. I THINK YOU MIGHT HAVE WHAT IT TAKES. THE LOOKS, THE CHARISMA, THE ATHLETICISM...
I'VE NEVER WRESTLED, GREG. WHAT WOULD I HAVE TO DO?
THAT WON'T BE A PROBLEM. HERE'S THE DEAL...
THE AWA SPONSORS A WRESTLING CAMP THAT RUNS FOR SIX WEEKS. YOU'LL BE COACHED BY ONE OF THE BEST, BILLY ROBINSON.

IT WAS 1972 AND I WAS ENROLLED WITH THE AMERICAN WRESTLING ASSOCIATION, TRAINING ALONGSIDE MEN WHO WOULD BECOME SOME OF THE BIGGEST NAMES IN THE INDUSTRY, INCLUDING...
...UNITED STATES OLYMPIC WEIGHTLIFTER, KEN PATERA...
...FUTURE 16-TIME WORLD CHAMPION, THE NATURE BOY, RIC FLAIR...
...AND MY FORMER GOLDEN GOPHER TEAMMATE AND FUTURE TAG TEAM PARTNER, GREG GAGNE.
AWA

ROBINSON WAS A TOUGH INSTRUCTOR. IT WAS LITERALLY A PROFESSIONAL WRESTLING BOOT CAMP. WE WOULD BEGIN WITH CALISTHENICS, WHICH INCLUDED 1,000 FREE SQUATS...
....FOLLOWED BY IN-RING INSTRUCTION ON GRAPPLING, BREAK FALLS, SUBMISSION HOLDS, AND HITTING THE ROPES.
WE LITERALLY BEAT THE STUFFING OUT OF EACH OTHER FOR SIX HOURS A DAY, SIX DAYS A WEEK. BUT I SURVIVED. I WAS NOW A MEMBER OF THE AWA.

MOOREHEAD, MINNESOTA.
DECEMBER 27, 1972
IN MY FIRST MATCH, I FACED 1971 AWA ROOKIE OF THE YEAR, DENNIS STAMP, IN A GRUELING, 15-MINUTE MATCH, ENDING IN A TIME-LIMIT DRAW.

...AND I WAS DISGUSTED WITH MY PERFORMANCE.
ITH OKAY, JIMMY.
YOU'RE GOING TO HAVE A LOT OF STINKERS IN YOUR CAREER. LEARN FROM EACH ONE!

ONCE I HAD MY FIRST "STINKER" UNDER MY BELT, I WAS READY FOR MY FIRST WIN, AGAINST STAN "KRUSHER" KOWALSKI.

KOWALSKI WAS A TOUGH COMPETITOR...

...A FORMER AWA WORLD TAG TEAM CHAMPION AS ONE-HALF OF MURDER, INCORPORATED.

BUT I SECURED THE VICTORY...
...AND EARNED MY FIRST PAYCHECK AS A PROFESSIONAL WRESTLER...$650.00.

IN 1973, ON THE INSTRUCTIONS OF VERNE GAGNE, I DEPARTED THE AWA FOR KANSAS CITY, MISSOURI, TO PERFORM FOR PROMOTER GUST KARRAS AND THE NWA CENTRAL STATES PROMOTION.
MISSOURI
Welcomes You
JIM, I WANT YOU TO MEET MIKE GEORGE. HE'S JUST IN FROM EDDIE GRAHAM'S PROMOTION DOWN IN FLORIDA. I WANT TO PAIR THE TWO OF YOU TOGETHER. TWO YOUNG, GOOD-LOOKING GUYS, I THINK YOU COULD WORK SOME MAGIC AS A TEAM.
I WAS ON THE WAY TO MY FIRST TAG TEAM TITLE CHAMPIONSHIP.

KANSAS CITY, MISSOURI.
OCTOBER 25, 1973
NWA CENTRAL STATES TAG TEAM CHAMPIONSHIP.
WE WERE FACING THE NWA CENTRAL STATE TAG TEAM CHAMPIONS, ROGER KIRBY AND LORD ALFRED HAYES, WITH THE TITLES ON THE LINE.
AFTER A HARD FOUGHT BATTLE, WE HAD DONE IT. MIKE AND I WERE THE CENTRAL STATES TAG TEAM CHAMPIONS, TITLES WE WOULD HOLD TWICE DURING MY STAY IN THE CENTRAL STATES PROMOTION.

MY TIME IN KANSAS CITY WASN'T SOLELY ABOUT WINNING CHAMPIONSHIPS, HOWEVER. IT WAS ALSO ABOUT LEARNING THE BUSINESS, AND I WAS LEARNING FROM SOME OF THE BEST.
MULTI-TIME CHAMPION AND ONE OF THE TOUGHEST MEN IN THE BUSINESS, HARLEY RACE.

WO-TIME NWA WORLD HEAVYWEIGHT
HAMPION, JACK BRISCO.

FOR TEN MONTHS, WHILE ALSO REIGNING AS A TAG TEAM CHAMPION, I STUDIED THE VETERANS, LEARNING THE INS AND OUTS OF THE PROFESSION.
THEN, IN 1974, THE CALL CAME. VERNE WAS SENDING ME TO JAPAN AND THE AJPW. MORE TRAINING. MORE LEARNING.

JAPAN
EVERY MATCH IN JAPAN WAS A FIGHT, A *LITERAL* FIGHT FOR YOUR LIFE.
I WAS MAKING $900 PER WEEK, AFTER VERNE TOOK HIS SHARE, AND I WAS LEARNING, GAINING VALUABLE EXPERIENCE.
SOON, I WOULD BE HEADED HOME TO THE AWA, BUT NOT BEFORE A LAYOVER IN HAWAII, ONE OF THE PERKS FOR WORKING WITH VERNE.

HAWAII WAS A FAVORITE STOP OF THE WRESTLERS WORKING FOR THE AWA AT THE TIME, THE PERFECT LAYOVER BETWEEN THE CONTINENTAL UNITED STATES AND JAPAN.
BRUNZELL!?! JIMMY BRUNZELL?!? TELEPHONE CALL FOR YOU!
IT WAS ON THIS LAYOVER THAT I RECEIVED A CALL THAT WOULD EVENTUALLY PROPEL ME TO SUPERSTAR STATUS IN THE AWA.
HEY, VERNE! JUST HAVING A LITTLE FUN WITH THE GUYS.
GOOD TO HEAR, JIMMY. GOOD TO HEAR. LISTEN, I NEED YOU TO GET BACK TO MINNESOTA. I'VE GOT SOMETHING LINED UP FOR YOU.
SURE, VERNE. WHAT HAVE YOU GOT?
I'M HERE WITH GREG. I THINK THE TWO OF YOU ARE READY FOR A TITLE RUN IN THE AWA. WE'RE GOING TO MAKE USE OF THOSE HIGH FLYING SKILLS OF YOURS. WHAT DO YOU THINK ABOUT A RUN AS "THE HIGH FLYERS"?

WITH THAT PHONE CALL IN 1975, THE HIGH FLYERS WERE BORN, AND I WAS PARTNERED WITH MY COLLEGE FOOTBALL TEAMMATE, GREG GAGNE, WHO HAD ESTABLISHED HIMSELF AS A STAR IN THE AWA.
WE QUICKLY BECAME FAN FAVORITES AND ESTABLISHED THE HIGH FLYERS AS ONE OF THE TOP TEAMS IN THE AWA...
...IN FEUDS AGAINST THE TEAM OF NICK BOCK-WINKEL AND RAY "THE CRIPPLER" STEVENS...
...AND THE TEAM OF LARS ANDERSON AND BUDDY WOLFE.

MANITOBA, WINNIPEG, CANADA. JULY 7, 1977
AWA WORLD TAG TEAM CHAMPIONSHIP.
BUT WE WERE TRAINED TO BE CHAMPIONS, AND, ON JULY 7, 1977, WE GOT THAT CHANCE AGAINST AWA WORLD TAG TEAM CHAMPIONS, BLACKJACK LANZA AND BOBBY DUNCUM.
THE MATCH WAS INTENSE, SEESAWING BACK-AND-FORTH BETWEEN US AND THE GIANTS IN BLACK.
BUT IN THE END, LANZA SUCCUMBED TO GREG'S SLEEPER HOLD, AND WE WERE THE NEW AWA TAG TEAM CHAMPIONS...TITLES WE WOULD HOLD FOR 443 DAYS, UNTIL I SUSTAINED AN INJURY OUTSIDE THE RING.

WELCOME TO NORTH CAROLINA
MY UNEXPECTED INJURY COST US THE TITLES, BUT IT OPENED MY EYES TO UNEXPLORED OPPORTUNITIES. FOR THREE YEARS, I BATTLED AS A MEMBER OF THE HIGH FLYERS.

I WAS READY TO EMERGE FROM THAT SHADOW AND TRY MY HAND AT SINGLES COMPETITION, SO I HIT THE ROAD TO CHARLOTTE, NORTH CAROLINA AND NWA MID-ATLANTIC PROMOTION.
IT WAS BRISTLING WITH EXCITEMENT AND FEATURED SOME OF THE MOST DYNAMIC WRESTLERS IN THE INDUSTRY, INCLUDING RIC FLAIR AND RICKY STEAMBOAT...

...AND BLACKJACK MULLIGAN AND JIMMY SNUKA.

I WAS WRESTLING EVERY DAY AND TWICE ON SATURDAYS.

RICHMOND, VIRGNIA.
SEPTEMBER 14, 1979
MY PERSISTENCE PAID OFF, EARNING ME THE MID-ATLANTIC HEAVYWEIGHT CHAMPIONSHIP ON TWO OCCASIONS, THE FIRST IN A VICTORY OVER KEN PATERA...
CHARLOTTE, NORTH CAROLINA.
CHRISTMAS DAY, 1979
...AND THE SECOND IN A WIN OVER RAY "THE CRIPPLER" STEVENS.

FOLLOWING MY SUCCESSFUL SINGLES RUN IN THE MID-ATLANTIC TERRITORY, AND AFTER SHORT SOJOURNS IN ATLANTA AND JAPAN, IT WAS TIME TO COME HOME...
....HOME TO THE AWA AND HOME TO THE HIGH FLYERS AND GREG GAGNE.
1981 WAS A GREAT YEAR. THE HIGH FLYERS LEAPT TO THE TOP OF THE TAG TEAM RANKS...
...SNATCHING THE AWA TAG TEAM CHAMPIONSHIP FROM THE EAST-WEST CONNECTION, COMPOSED OF JESSE VENTURA AND ADRIAN ADONIS, HOLDING THE BELTS FOR AN AWA RECORD 742 DAYS.
THE MONEY WAS GREAT...
...AS WERE THE PERKS.
"THE BOSS" BRUCE SPRINGSTEEN.

BUT, BY 1982, THE AWA WAS SUFFERING, ATTENDANCE WAS IN DECLINE, AND THE WWF WAS ON THE HORIZON. THE COMPANY, BEHIND THE LEADERSHIP OF THE MCMAHON FAMILY, WAS ACQUIRING THE TOP TALENT FROM THE COMPETING ORGANIZATIONS AND TERRITORIES...INCLUDING THE AWA.
THAT'S WHEN I WENT TO VERNE GAGNE.
VERNE, I LOVE THE AWA. I LOVE WHAT YOU'VE DONE FOR ME. I LOVE BEING GREG'S PARTNER WITH THE HIGH FLYERS, BUT I'VE GOT A FAMILY...EXPENSES. I NEED MORE MONEY TO STAY. A CONTRACT.
WHAT ARE WE LOOKING AT, JIMMY?
NINETY-FIVE THOUSAND, GUARANTEED. THAT'S WHAT IT'S GOING TO TAKE.
SORRY, JIMMY. I CAN'T DO IT. YOU'RE JUST NOT WORTH IT.
AND WITH THAT...I WAS GONE. A QUICK PHONE CALL TO MY FRIEND TERRY BOLLEA, BETTER KNOWN BY HIS RING NAME "HULK HOGAN", WHO RECENTLY LEFT THE AWA FOR THE WWF, AND I WAS ON MY WAY TO NEW YORK CITY TO COMPETE IN SINGLES COMPETITION FOR THE WWF.
...SOUNDS GOOD TERRY. PLEASE THANK GEORGE SCOTT FOR ME.

JIMMY, I NEED TO TALK TO YOU, BROTHER. THERE'S A GUY I WANT YOU TO MEET AT THE SHOW IN BRANTFORD.
OH, YEAH? WHO'S THAT?
IT WAS AN EASY TRANSITION TO THE WWF. I WAS WINNING SINGLES MATCHES, BUT THERE JUST WASN'T THE "POP" I HAD AS A TAG TEAM WRESTLER WITH THE HIGH FLYERS...
A FRIEND OF MINE FROM MATSUDA'S GYM...BRIAN BLAIR. HE REMINDS ME A LOT OF YOU, ANOTHER HIGH FLYER.
YEAH? WHAT ARE YOU THINKING? TAG TEAM?
YEAH, BROTHER. YOU GUYS WOULD DRAW. THINK ABOUT IT.

Robert Gibson

The Developmental Years

Birth Name:	Ruben Cain
Born:	July 19, 1958 Pensacola, Florida
Height:	5' 11"
Weight:	224 lbs
Career:	1977-Present

The younger brother, sometime partner, and protege of Ricky Gibson, Ruben Cain first took the ring name Robert Gibson in 1977. Ricky was a popular wrestler in the Alabama and Tennessee territories before a head-on collision in 1980 led to career-ending injuries.

Prior to that tragedy, however, the brothers enjoyed substantial tag team success, winning the NWA Americas Tag Team Championship from The Twin Devils in 1979.

The brothers were raised in the Florida Panhandle, hearing children of parents who were both deaf. They were fluent in American sign language, and Robert has frequently been known to speak with his hands before matches. Ricky and Robert remained close after Ricky was forced to retire following the auto accident. In fact, in 1982, following a few years of Robert wrestling in singles competition in small promotions before even smaller crowds, he was introduced to Ricky Morton by his brother Ricky.

Legendary Memphis wrestler Jerry Lawler molded Morton and Gibson into the Rock 'n' Roll Express, launching one of the most over tag teams of the 1980's and one that continues to wrestle competitively in 2020. Their good looks, hair metal-loving personas, and high-flying style proved popular for the era, and they steadily elevated their profile in 1983 and 1984 by feuding with a series of tag teams, including Lanny Poffo and Randy Savage, before moving up to Mid-South Wrestling, where they engaged in their most famous matches with Jim Cornette's Midnight Express.

Ricky Morton

The Developmental Years

Art by Rich Perotta
& Vito Potenza

Born:	Sept. 21, 1956 Nashville, TN
Height:	5' 11"
Weight:	227 lbs
Career:	1978-Present

Ricky Morton is the son of Memphis-based wrestling referee, Paul Morton, offering him early opportunities to be a part of the industry, setting up prior to matches and attentively studying the performances of Jerry Lawler, among others. Initially considered too small to be a professional wrestler, Ricky's father and seasoned veteran, Ken Lucas, took him under their wings and trained him. In 1978, he competed in his first match against Ken Wayne, fighting to a time-limit draw over fifteen minutes.

Ricky and Ken Lucas frequently teamed in the Mid-South territory, until Ke suffered an injury in 1982, leading to Morton competing in televised Southwes Championship Wrestling singles competition against Tully Blanchard for the promo tion's Television Championship. That same night, he taped a second match agains The Grappler, Len Denton, and both contests were observed by American Wrestlin Association (AWA) World Heavyweight Champion, Nick Bockwinkel, and his man ager, Bobby "The Brain" Heenan. The pair were sufficiently impressed with his skill and performance that they scheduled Morton for an AWA World Heavyweigh Championship bout the very next week, and the competitors wrestled to hard-fought 60-minute draw.

The pair tangled in a 2-out-of-3 falls rematch in Houston on July 1, 1982, wit Morton scoring one fall but ultimately losing to Bockwinkel. The legend of the epi match spread quickly, warranting a call to Morton from Jerry Lawler, who recalle him to Memphis for the next phase of his career in the Rock 'n' Roll Express.

EXPRESS

RICKY MORTON

writer **John E. Crowther**
@crowman1971

artist **Rich Perotta**
@RichPerottaArt

colorist **Vito Potenza**
@PiwiTFP

letterer **Jessica Hinds**
@Jessapalooza

editor/designer **Kevin LaPorte**
@kevinlaporte

HALL OF FAME INDUCTION CEREMONY.
ORLANDO, FLORIDA – MARCH 31, 2017.
Amway CENTER
LADIES AND GENTLEMEN... *THE ROCK 'N' ROLL EXPRESS!*

WITH HARD WORK, IF YOU BELIEVE IN YOURSELF, YOU CAN ACCOMPLISH ANYTHING.
SCHOOL OF MORTON WRESTLING SCHOOL. CHUCKY, TENNESSEE – PRESENT DAY.
HOW'D YOU DO IT, *MR. MORTON?* HOW'D YOU MAKE IT FROM TENNESSEE TO THE *HALL OF FAME?*
WHERE DO I BEGIN?
PULL UP A SEAT.
LET'S ROCK 'N' ROLL.

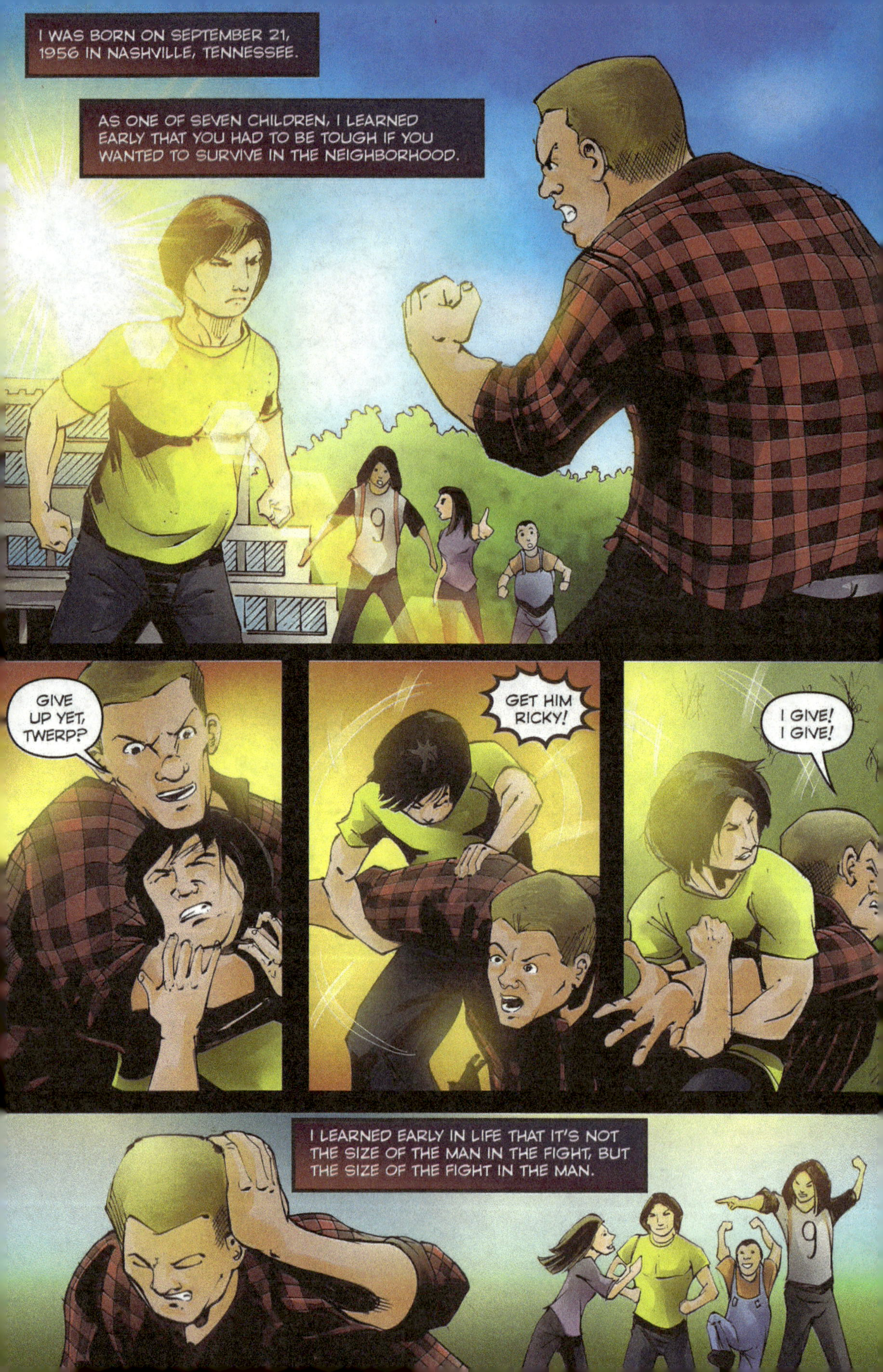

I WAS BORN ON SEPTEMBER 21, 1956 IN NASHVILLE, TENNESSEE.

AS ONE OF SEVEN CHILDREN, I LEARNED EARLY THAT YOU HAD TO BE TOUGH IF YOU WANTED TO SURVIVE IN THE NEIGHBORHOOD.

GIVE UP YET, TWERP?

GET HIM RICKY!

I GIVE! I GIVE!

FOR YEARS, MY FATHER, *PAUL MORTON*, WAS A STAPLE IN MEMPHIS WRESTLING AS A REFEREE.

HE WAS A STICKLER FOR THE RULES AND NEVER BACKED DOWN IN THE RING.

HE CALLED THEM HOW HE SAW THEM...

....AND STOOD AMONG CHAMPIONS, SUCH AS CWA WORLD CHAMPION, *JERRY LAWLER*.

I IDOLIZED MY FATHER, IN AWE OF THE ARENAS AND STARS OF THE SQUARED CIRCLE.
MEMPHIS, TENNESSEE.
I WOULD ASSIST IN SETTING UP THE RING PRIOR TO MATCHES...
...AND WOULD STUDY THE MATCHES WITH UNBRIDLED ATTENTION.

I DIDN'T WANT TO BE A BYSTANDER OR TO MERELY WORK BEHIND THE SCENES. I WANTED A PIECE OF THE ACTION.
HEY, DAD. CAN YOU TRAIN ME? I THINK I CAN TAKE SOME OF THESE GUYS.
STICK TO THE *SIDELINES*, KID. YOU'RE TOO SMALL FOR THIS SPORT.
IGNORE HIM, SON. YOU'RE A *MORTON*.
YOU CAN BE A CHAMP IN THIS BUSINESS. KEN AND I WILL TRAIN YOU.

BY "KEN", MY FATHER REFERRED TO KEN LUCAS, ONE OF MY FIRST TAG TEAM PARTNERS AND THE HOLDER OF MULTIPLE CHAMPIONSHIP TITLES THROUGHOUT THE NWA TERRITORIES DURING THE 60'S, 70'S, AND 80'S.
THEY TAUGHT ME HOW TO TAKE A BUMP...
...HOW TO THROW A PROPER PUNCH...
...AND HOW TO LAND MY AERIAL MANEUVERS.
I WAS READY FOR MY FIRST MATCH.

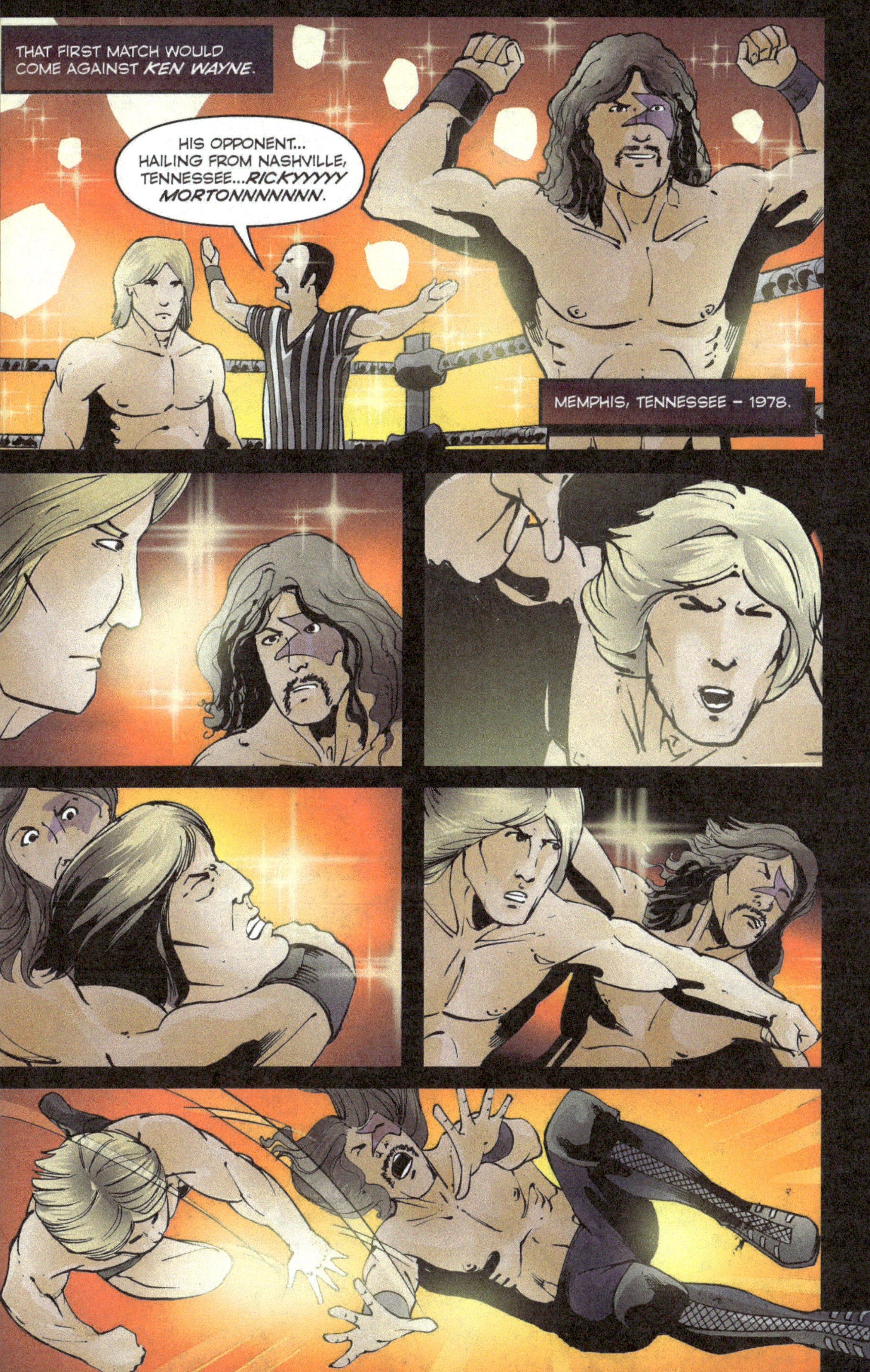
THAT FIRST MATCH WOULD COME AGAINST *KEN WAYNE*.
HIS OPPONENT... HAILING FROM NASHVILLE, TENNESSEE...*RICKYYYYY MORTONNNNNNN*.
MEMPHIS, TENNESSEE – 1978.

IT WAS A HARD-FOUGHT MATCH, WITH NEITHER ME NOR KEN GAINING A DISTINCT ADVANTAGE.
AFTER 15 GRUELING MINUTES I FINISHED MY FIRST PROFESSIONAL MATCH, A 15-MINUTE TIME LIMIT DRAW AGAINST A SOLID OPPONENT.

MID-SOUTH COLISEUM
MEMPHIS, TENNESSEE.
WITH MY FIRST MATCH UNDER MY BELT, I WAS SET TO MAKE A NAME FOR MYSELF IN MID-SOUTHERN WRESTLING...
BOTH AS A SINGLES COMPETITOR...

TAG!
...AND AS A TAG TEAM COMPETITOR WITH MY FORMER TRAINER, KEN LUCAS...

...AND ANOTHER DYNAMIC AND RISING STAR..."HOT STUFF" EDDIE GILBERT.

SAN ANTONIO, TEXAS.
IN 1982, I WAS WRESTLING IN SAN ANTONIO, TEXAS, FOR SOUTHWEST CHAMPIONSHIP WRESTLING, A PROMOTION HEADED BY JOE BLANCHARD. MY TAG TEAM PARTNER, KEN LUCAS, HAD BEEN INJURED. AN OPPORTUNITY THAT WOULD CHANGE THE COURSE OF MY CAREER WAS SET INTO MOTION.
JOE, WITH KEN OUT, I NEED A NEW TAG TEAM PARTNER. DO YOU HAVE ANYONE IN MIND?
RICKY, I'VE GOT ANOTHER IDEA.
WE'RE DOING SOME TV TAPINGS AT HEMISFAIR ARENA NEXT WEEK. HOW DO YOU FEEL ABOUT FILMING A COUPLE MATCHES AGAINST THE GRAPPLER AND TULLY? IT'LL BE A GREAT WAY TO BUILD ON YOUR BABYFACE IMAGE.
LET'S DO IT!

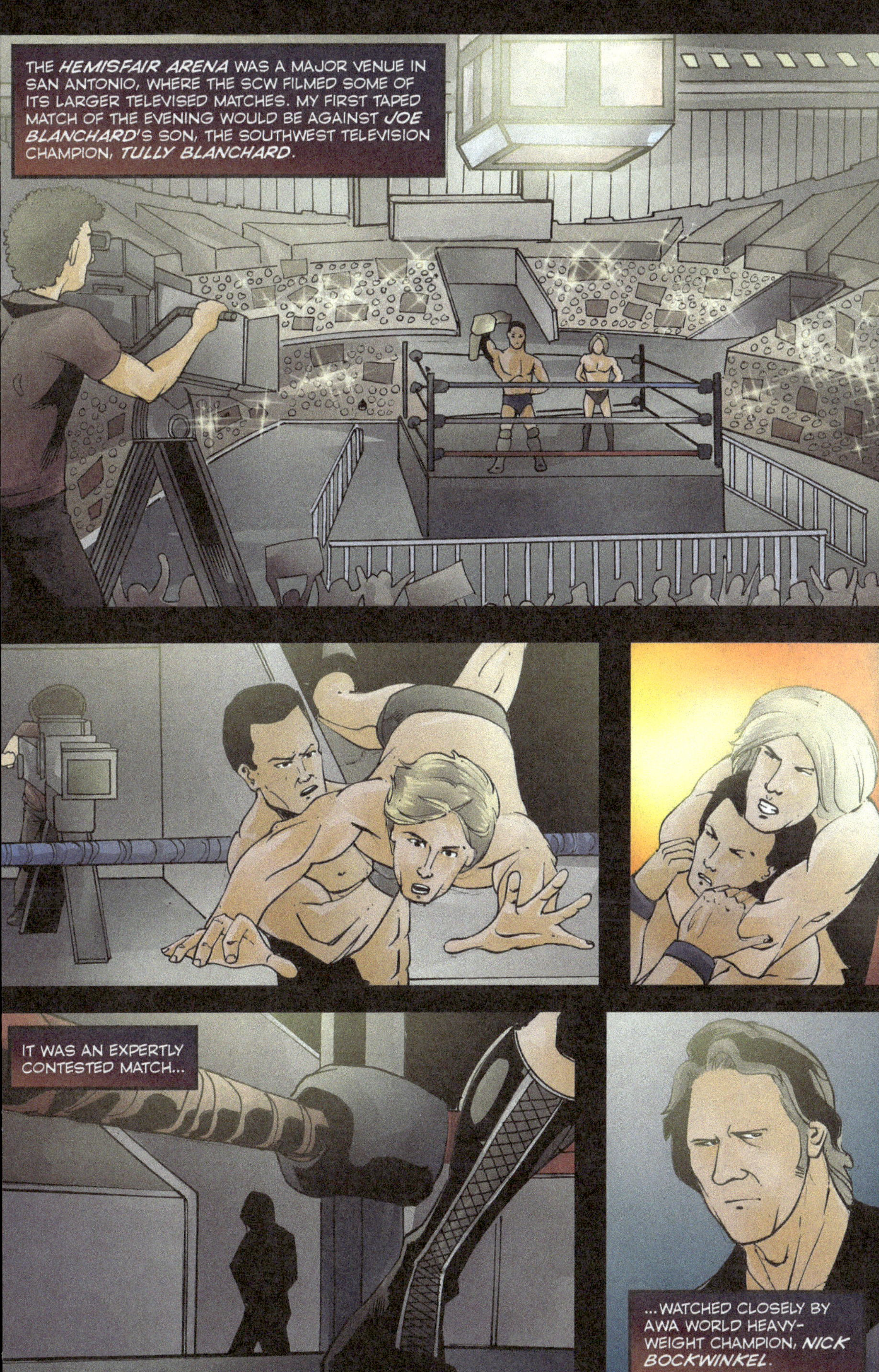
THE HEMISFAIR ARENA WAS A MAJOR VENUE IN SAN ANTONIO, WHERE THE SCW FILMED SOME OF ITS LARGER TELEVISED MATCHES. MY FIRST TAPED MATCH OF THE EVENING WOULD BE AGAINST JOE BLANCHARD'S SON, THE SOUTHWEST TELEVISION CHAMPION, TULLY BLANCHARD.
IT WAS AN EXPERTLY CONTESTED MATCH...
...WATCHED CLOSELY BY AWA WORLD HEAVY-WEIGHT CHAMPION, NICK BOCKWINKEL.

THE SECOND MATCH I TAPED THAT NIGHT WAS AGAINST *THE GRAPPLER, LEN DENTON*.
THIS MATCH WAS ALSO WATCHED BY THE AWA CHAMPION...
...BUT NOW HE WAS JOINED BY HIS MANAGER, *BOBBY "THE BRAIN" HEENAN*.

MY TAPINGS COMPLETE, I STUCK AROUND TO SEE THE CHAMP AND HIS MATCH AGAINST A GAME SCOTT CASEY.
YOUR AWA WORLD HEAVYWEIGHT CHAMPION... NICK BOCKWINKEL! ACCOMPANYING MR. BOCKWINKEL TO THE RING IS HIS MANAGER, BOBBY "THE BRAIN" HEENAN!
BOOOO!
WEASEL!
THE CHAMP WAS TECHNICALLY SOUND IN THE RING.
I STUDIED HIM CLOSELY.
THE CHAMP SECURED HIS WIN, AND I SOAKED IT ALL IN.

WHAT'S YOUR NAME, BOY?
I'M RICKY MORTON.
MORTON? I'M BOBBY HEENAN. ARE YOU PAUL MORTON'S SON?
YEAH.
I KNOW YOUR DAD.
I JUST WATCHED YOUR MATCH. YOU DID GREAT. YOU'VE GOT GREAT TIMING. YOU DID AN EXCELLENT JOB SELLING THE STORY AND THE MATCH.
ME AND THE CHAMP. WE'VE GOT OUR EYES ON YOU, RICKY.

SEVERAL DAYS LATER.
HEY, RICKY. CHECK THIS OUT. DID YOU SEE THE CARD FOR THE BIG EVENT NEXT WEEKEND IN HEMISFAIR?
NAH... WHO'S IN IT?
DID I MAKE THE CARD?
MAKE THE CARD? RICKY...YOU'RE IN THE MAIN EVENT.
THE MAIN EVENT? I'VE GOT A SHOT AT THE TITLE!

HEMISFAIR ARENA - SAN ANTONIO, TEXAS.
I HAD EARNED MY FIRST SHOT AT THE *AWA WORLD HEAVYWEIGHT CHAMPIONSHIP* AGAINST *NICK BOCKWINKEL* IN FRONT OF A SELLOUT CROWD OF 30,000 SCREAMING FANS.
HIS OPPONENT...YOUR *AWA WORLD HEAVYWEIGHT CHAMPION*...ACCOMPANIED TO THE RING BY HIS MANAGER, *BOBBY "THE BRAIN" HEENAN*...NICK *BOCKWINKEL!*
IT WASN'T JUST GOING TO BE A BATTLE. IT WAS GOING TO BE A BATTLE OF ENDURANCE.
DING DING

WE BATTLED FOR 60 MINUTES, NEITHER MAN ABLE TO CLAIM A DISTINCT ADVANTAGE.
NEITHER MAN SCORED A SUBMISSION OR A PIN FALL.
THIS MATCH IS DECLARED A DRAW!
STILL AWA WORLD HEAVYWEIGHT CHAMPION... NICK BOCKWINKEL.
I DIDN'T CAPTUR THE CHAMPIONSHIP BELT, BUT I CAPTURED THE ATTENTION OF THE CHAMPION AND OF HOUSTON PROMOTER, PAUL BOESCH.

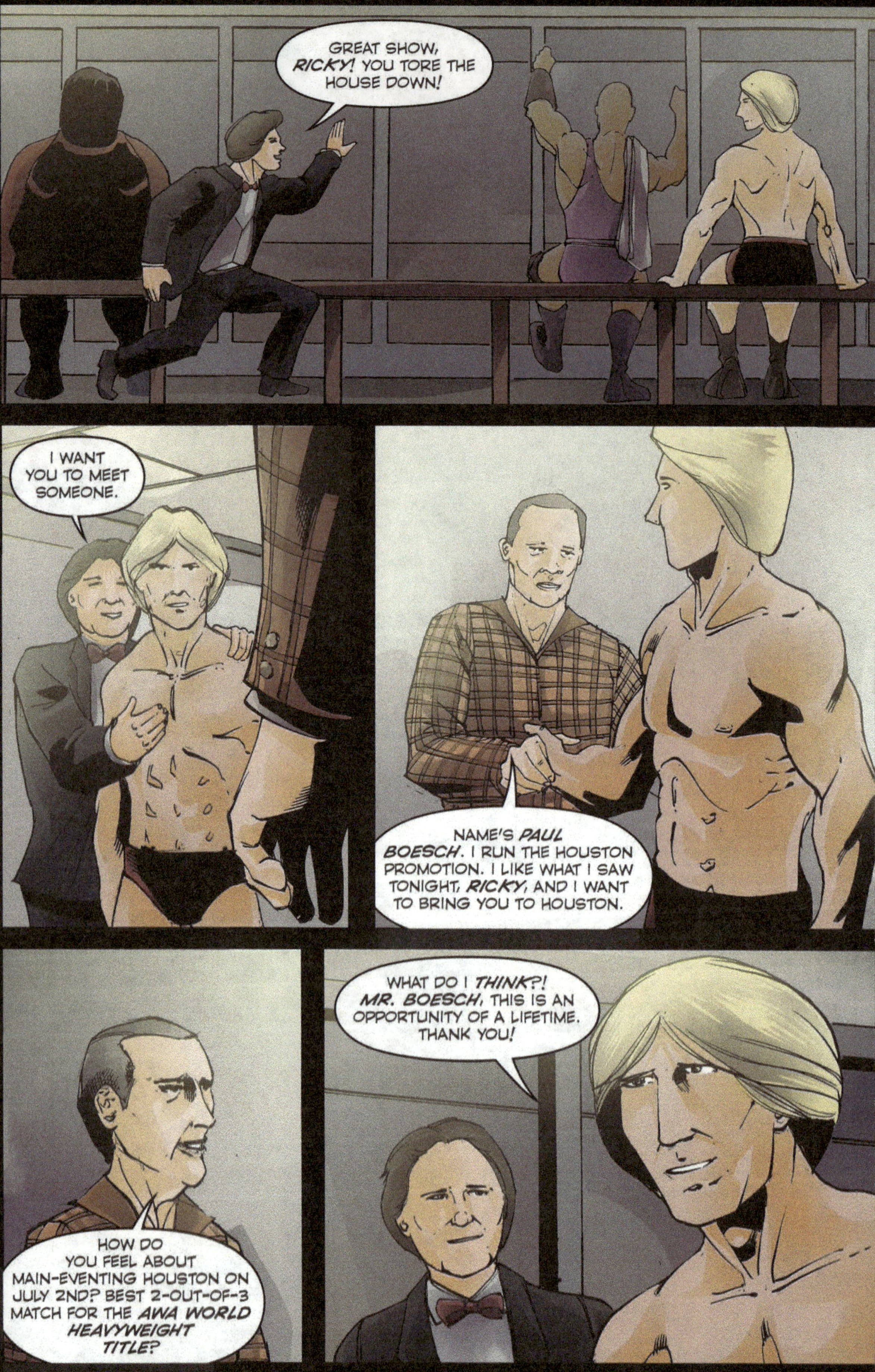

GREAT SHOW, *RICKY!* YOU TORE THE HOUSE DOWN!

I WANT YOU TO MEET SOMEONE.

NAME'S *PAUL BOESCH*. I RUN THE HOUSTON PROMOTION. I LIKE WHAT I SAW TONIGHT, *RICKY*, AND I WANT TO BRING YOU TO HOUSTON.

HOW DO YOU FEEL ABOUT MAIN-EVENTING HOUSTON ON JULY 2ND? BEST 2-OUT-OF-3 MATCH FOR THE *AWA WORLD HEAVYWEIGHT TITLE?*

JULY 1, 1982.
BEFORE A SOLD OUT CROWD AT THE SAM HOUSTON COLISEUM. I HAD A REMATCH FOR THE AWA WORLD HEAVYWEIGHT TITLE.
YOUR CHAMPION, ACCOMPANIED TO THE RING BY HIS MANAGER, BOBBY HEENAN...NICK BOCKWINKLE!!!
AND HIS CHALLENGER, HAILING FROM NASHVILLE, TENNESSEE... RICKY MORTON!
WE SIZED EACH OTHER UP FROM ACROSS THE RING.
A 2-OUT-OF-3 MATCH FOR THE CHAMPIONSHIP. A CHANCE TO PROVE I WAS THE BEST IN THE WORLD.

THE MATCH QUICKLY BECAME AN INTENSE STRUGGLE, PITTING YOUTHFUL EXUBERANCE AND SPEED AGAINST VETERAN SAVVY AND STRENGTH.
IN THE SECOND FALL, REELING FROM THE PILE DRIVER, I KEPT MY DISTANCE, THEN LURED THE CHAMPION IN AND SNATCHED THE SECOND PINFALL WITH A PERFECTLY EXECUTED SUNSET FLIP.
BY NOW, AT THE VERGE OF EXHAUSTION, EACH OF US BROUGHT THE BATTLE TO THE OTHER, HOPING FOR THE PERFECT MOVE, OR FATAL MISTAKE, THAT WOULD SEAL THE VICTORY.

EARLY IN THE MATCH, I FRUSTRATED THE CHAMPION WITH MY SPEED, ESCAPING HIS CLUTCH TIME AND AGAIN.

BUT A CARELESS MISTAKE FOUND ME VICTIM OF A PILE DRIVER AND LOSER OF THE FIRST FALL.

I MADE THAT MISTAKE, MISSING A FLYING CROSS BODY, AND THE VETERAN BOCKWINKLE CAPITALIZED, ROLLING ME UP FOR THE THIRD PINFALL AND RETAINING HIS CHAMPIONSHIP.

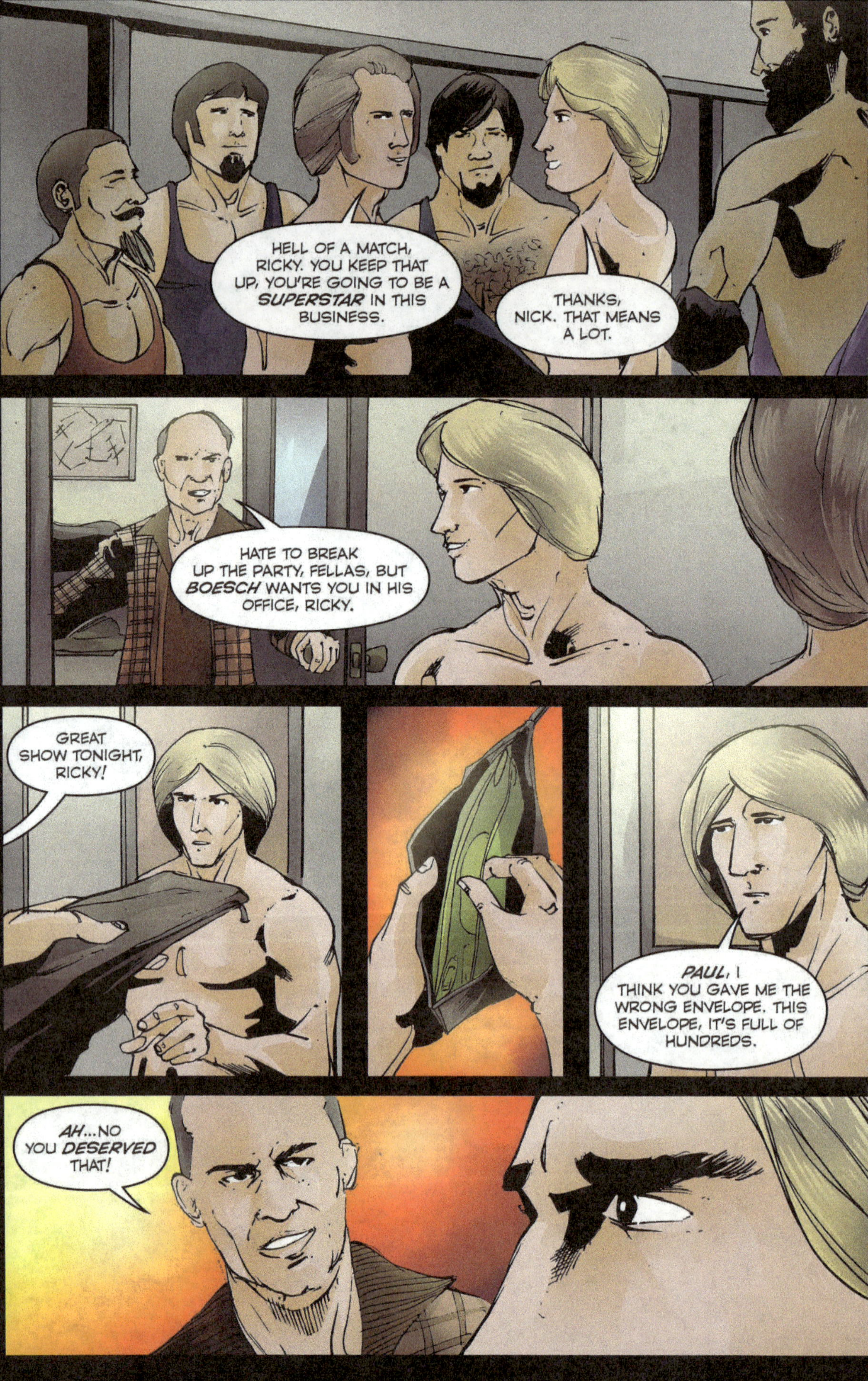
HELL OF A MATCH, RICKY. YOU KEEP THAT UP, YOU'RE GOING TO BE A *SUPERSTAR* IN THIS BUSINESS.
THANKS, NICK. THAT MEANS A LOT.
HATE TO BREAK UP THE PARTY, FELLAS, BUT *BOESCH* WANTS YOU IN HIS OFFICE, RICKY.
GREAT SHOW TONIGHT, RICKY!
PAUL, I THINK YOU GAVE ME THE WRONG ENVELOPE. THIS ENVELOPE, IT'S FULL OF HUNDREDS.
AH...NO YOU *DESERVED* THAT!

I RECEIVED $2,800 FOR A SINGLE MATCH. PRIOR TO THAT NIGHT, I HAD NEVER EARNED MORE THAN A COUPLE HUNDRED FOR A MATCH, BUT MY FORTUNES WERE ABOUT TO CHANGE.
BUH-RING BUH-RING
THIS IS RICKY MORTON.
RICKY! JERRY LAWLER. HEARD ABOUT YOUR MATCH TONIGHT. MEET ME IN SAN ANTONIO. WE NEED TO TALK.
CONTINUED.

Ric Flair

The Nature Boy

Birth Name: Richard Fliehr
Born: February 25, 1949
Memphis, TN
Daughter: Charlotte Flair
Height: 6' 1"
Weight: 243 lbs
Career: 1972-2012

Art by Amanda Rachels

The infant who would become arguably the greatest professional wrestler of all time was abandoned by his biological parents and cared for by the Tennessee Children's Home Society, which was a front for a long-running baby trafficking operation run by Georgia Tann. He was adopted by Dr. Richard and Kathleen Fliehr, and the family soon relocated to Edina, Minnesota, where young Richard was raised and participated in high school wrestling.

After graduation, he began training with Great Lakes regional wrestling promoter, Verne Gagne, at a camp held in Gagne's barn and including Gagne's son, Greg, Jim Brunzell, The Iron Sheik, and Ken Patera. He made his professional wrestling debut under the name Ric Flair in Gagne's American Wrestling Association (AWA) in 1972 and squared off against such legends as Dusty Rhodes and Andre the Giant while with the promotion. His first title belt was the Mid-Atlantic TV Championship, which he won from Paul Jones in 1975 after transferring to the National Wrestling Alliance's (NWA's) Mid-Atlantic territory.

Later that year, while on a flight to an NWA show, the plane crashed in Wilmington, North Carolina, a catastrophe Flair survived but with a back broken in three places. Told by doctors he would never wrestle again, he returned to the ring in just eight months, transitioning, out of medical necessity, from a brawling style to a more technical methodology that, in combination with his Nature Boy persona affected in a 1978 rivalry with original Nature Boy, Buddy Rogers, launched him to superstardom

Beginning July 29, 1977, Flair held the NWA United States Heavyweight Championship for five separate runs, beginning with a win over Bobo Brazil and later involving feuds with Ricky "The Dragon" Steamboat, Roddy Piper, Jimmy Snuka, and Greg "The Hammer" Valentine.

This streak of success was mere practice for what was to come. In 1981, Flair defeated frequent rival Dusty Rhodes for the NWA World Heavyweight Championship, and he would lose and win it back eight more times through 1991. He was successfully pinned for the title at various times by all-time greats, Harley Race, Kerry Von Erich, Ron Garvin, Sting, and previous belt-holder Dusty Rhodes, but, in each instance, he regained the title via rematch in short order.

In 1985, Flair's support from the fraternal tag team of Arn and Ole Anderson developed into perhaps the most renowned pro wrestling stable ever seen in the industry, The Four Horsemen, when Tully Blanchard joined forces with them to terrorize the NWA and to monopolize its title belts while devastating Dusty Rhodes, Magnum TA, and others.

Flair was briefly both NWA World Heavyweight Champion and World Championship Wrestling (WCW) Heavyweight Champion, but a dispute with WCW President Jim Herd forced him out of the new promotion and to the World Wrestling Federation (WWF), causing him to also ultimately vacate the NWA belt. He won the 1992 Royal Rumble to claim his first WWF Championship, only to lose it to The Macho Man Randy Savage at WrestleMania VII after a feud in which Flair claimed to have had a prior relationship with Miss Elizabeth. He returned to WCW after losing a Loser Leaves the WWF match to Mr. Perfect in January, 1993.

His extended second run in WCW included multiple reigns as Heavyweight Champion, feuds between The Four Horsemen and the New World Order (nWo), and a gimmick involving him as the on-air President of WCW. When that promotion was absorbed by the WWF, Flair returned and later formed Evolution with Triple H, Randy Orton, and Batista. He was inducted into the WWE Hall of Fame in 2008.

writer John E. Crowther
@crowman1971

artist Javier Lugo
@jlugo627

colorist Blake Wilkie
@Tecracoon

editor/designer Kevin LaPorte
@kevinlaporte

MARY LOU PATTON PARK,
CHILLICOTHE, OHIO. 1969.
GET'EM, JIMMY!!!
GO, JIMMY!!!

I WASN'T ALWAYS *'FANTASTIC' BOBBY FULTON*. I WAS BORN *JAMES FRANKLIN HINES* ON OCTOBER 4, 1960, IN CHILLI-COTHE, OHIO.

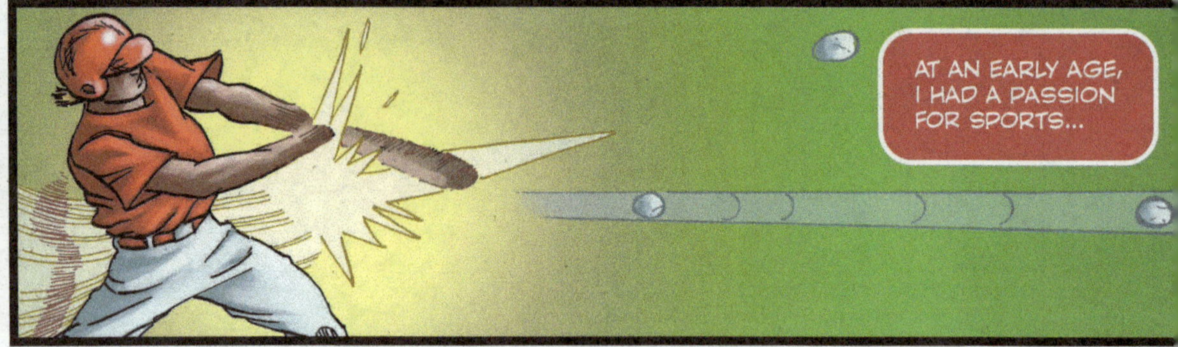
AT AN EARLY AGE, I HAD A PASSION FOR SPORTS...

...AND AN INHERENT KNACK FOR WINNING.

BILL FETTERS WAS MY LITTLE LEAGUE BASEBALL COACH AND A MAJOR INFLUENCE IN THOSE EARLY YEARS.
GREAT GAME, JIMMY. CAN I GIVE YOU A LIFT HOME?
SURE, COACH.
PUT YOUR GEAR IN BACK AND HOP IN, CHAMP.

FOR AS LONG AS I COULD REMEMBER, I WANTED TO BE A PROFESSIONAL WRESTLER.

SO, JIMMY, WHADDA YOU WANNA BE WHEN YOU GROW UP? YOU GONNA BE A PROFESSIONAL BALL PLAYER?
NAH, COACH. A PROFESSIONAL WRESTLER. YEAH... I'M GONNA BE A ***PROFESSIONAL WRESTLER***.

SEE YA TOMORROW, JIMMY!

ANOTHER EARLY INFLUENCE ON MY LIFE WAS THE LORD, OUR SAVIOR, *JESUS CHRIST*.

I BECAME A CHRISTIAN AT THE AGE OF 11 AND WAS DEVOUT IN MY ATTENDANCE AND MY FAITH.

BUT AS DEDICATED AS I WAS TO MY CHRISTIAN BELIEFS, I WAS EQUALLY DEDICATED TO MY LOVE OF PROFESSIONAL WRESTLING...

...RUNNING 13 BLOCKS, EVERY SUNDAY, FROM THE OPEN BIBLE BAPTIST CHURCH TO MY HOME TO WATCH PROFESSIONAL WRESTLING ON THE FAMILY TELEVISION.

I WAS ENGROSSED BY THE TELEVISED MATCHES PUT ON BY EDWARD FARHAT'S *BIG TIME WRESTLING*, BASED IN DETROIT, MICHIGAN AND AIRED IN CHILLICOTHE ON CHANNEL 22, OUT OF DAYTON, OHIO.

FARHAT, ONE OF THE ORIGINATORS OF HARDCORE WRESTLING, WAS KNOWN IN THE WRESTLING RING AS 'THE SHEIK' OR 'THE ORIGINAL SHEIK', TO DISTINGUISH HIM FROM 'THE IRON SHEIK', WHO DEBUTED SEVERAL YEARS LATER.

THE SHEIK WAS FAMED FOR HIS VIOLENT FEUDS WITH SUCH GREATS AS BOBO BRAZIL...

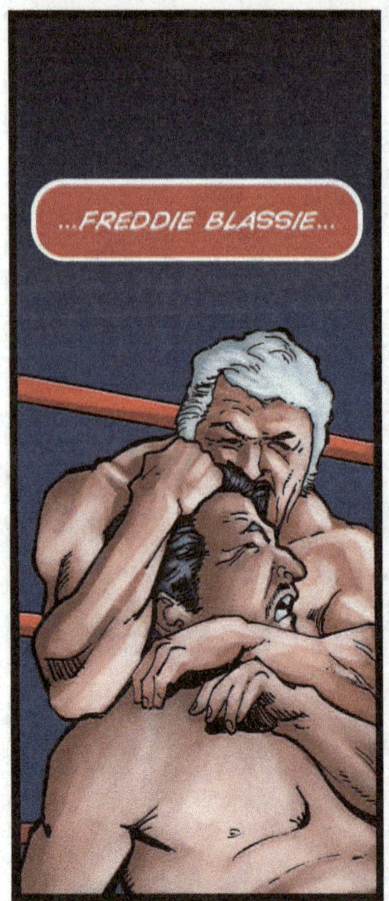
...FREDDIE BLASSIE...

...ANDRE THE GIANT...

...AND BRUNO SAMMARTINO.
AND THE SHEIK BROUGHT THIS HARDCORE STYLE OF WRESTLING TO HIS BIG TIME WRES-TLING PROMOTION.

I WAS *TRANSFIXED* BY THE WRESTLERS' PERFORMANCES AND THE SOUNDS OF THE MATCHES. THE *THUMPING* OF THE RING, THE *ROAR* OF THE CROWD, THE *POUNDING* OF FISTS TO FLESH. IT WAS ORCHESTRAL...MESMERIZING...

ARENA
TELEVISED WRESTLING WASN'T ENOUGH FOR ME. I NEEDED TO BE A *PART* OF THE ACTION, *LIVE* AND IN PERSON. SO, AT THE AGE OF 13, I BEGAN ASSISTING WITH AL HAFT'S WRESTLING PROMOTION...*THE MID-WEST WRESTLING ALLIANCE*.

...FIGHTING OUT OF FRANKLIN, OHIO...THE FIGHTING LINEMAN...*LEON GRAHAM!*
HAFT'S PROMOTION WAS LOADED WITH SUCH LOCAL TALENT AS *KILLER JD KENT*, *LEON GRAHAM*...

...AND THE INFAMOUS CONVICTED KILLER, *DR. SAM SHEPPARD*, WHO WAS FAMOUSLY PORTRAYED IN THE MOVIE, "*THE FUGITIVE*".
WHY ISN'T SAM SHEPPARD IN JAIL?

WRESTLING HAS ALWAYS BEEN A CLOSE FRATERNITY. IT WAS NOT EASY TO BREAK INTO THE INDUSTRY, PARTICULARLY FOR A 13-YEAR-OLD *KID* WITH NO TRAINING OR FAMILY IN THE BUSINESS. I HAD TO FIND A WAY IN...
HERE, KID! TAKE THESE TO THE LOCKER ROOM.

...AND I *DID*, BY ASSISTING WITH PRE- AND AFTER-SHOW DUTIES, INCLUDING SETTING UP AND DISMANTLING THE RINGS.

GOOD WORK, JIMMY.

BUT ASSISTING WITH THE SHOWS WAS TIME-CONSUMING, AND, WHILE IT PROVIDED ME WITH KNOWLEDGE ABOUT THE INNER WORKINGS OF THE INDUSTRY AND GAINED ME FRIENDS WITHIN ITS RANKS, IT LEFT LITTLE OR NO TIME FOR *ACTUAL* TRAINING.

HEY, KID. PUT DOWN THE BROOM.

AIN'T NOBODY EVER WON A *TITLE* BY SWEEPIN' A BROOM. LET ME SHOW YOU SOMETHIN'.

SO, MY INFORMAL TRAINING BEGAN. I BECAME A PART OF THE WRESTLING FAMILY.

WHEN I WASN'T SETTING UP RINGS, CARRYING EQUIPMENT, OR SWEEPING A BROOM, I WAS IN THE RING, LEARNING FROM EXPERIENCE...

...ROLLING ON THE MAT...

...LEARNING TECHNIQUES...

...AND BUILDING CONFIDENCE.

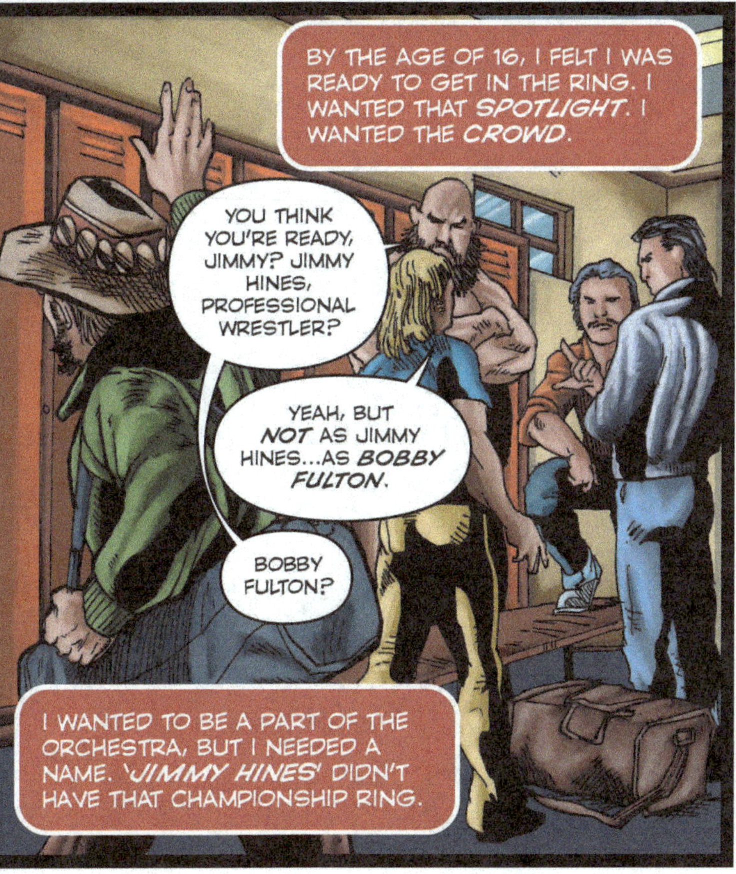
BY THE AGE OF 16, I FELT I WAS READY TO GET IN THE RING. I WANTED THAT SPOTLIGHT. I WANTED THE CROWD.
YOU THINK YOU'RE READY, JIMMY? JIMMY HINES, PROFESSIONAL WRESTLER?
YEAH, BUT NOT AS JIMMY HINES...AS BOBBY FULTON.
BOBBY FULTON?
I WANTED TO BE A PART OF THE ORCHESTRA, BUT I NEEDED A NAME. 'JIMMY HINES' DIDN'T HAVE THAT CHAMPIONSHIP RING.

UH-HUH. BOBBY FULTON. I LIKE THE SOUND OF IT.

MY LIFE AS BOBBY FULTON, PROFESSIONAL WRESTLER, WAS ABOUT TO BEGIN. I HAD NO FORMAL TRAINING, BUT I HAD A *NAME*, I HAD *DESIRE* AND, COURTESY OF MY PARENTS, I HAD A PAIR OF *K&H* ORIGINAL WRESTLING BOOTS. THE ONLY THING I NEEDED WAS AN *OPPONENT*.

SO, IN 1977, AT THE AGE OF 16, I SET OFF WITH MY FATHER, FOR MY FIRST OFFICIAL PROFESSIONAL WRESTLING MATCH.
YOU KNOW, JIMMY, PROFESSIONAL WRESTLING...IT'S NOT *REAL*.
IF IT AIN'T *REAL*, I AIN'T DOIN' IT.

THE MATCH WAS PART OF A *THREE RIVERS WRESTLING* SHOW IN CLARKSBURG, WEST VIRGINIA, AND HAD BEEN ARRANGED BY *KEN JUGAN*, A WRESTLER AND PROMOTER, KNOWN TO FANS AS *LORD ZOLTAN*.
YOU'D *BETTER* DO IT.

HOW OLD ARE YOU, KID? *SIXTEEN?* YOU'RE TOO *YOUNG* TO WRESTLE.
UM..I'M SEVENTEEN.
HEH...YEAH, WELL, WE'RE A BIT *SHORT*. YOU'RE IN THE SECOND MATCH. GET READY.

GIVE 'EM HELL, KID.

...HAILING FROM CHILLICOTHE, OHIO... BOBBY FULTON!

AND HIS OPPONENT... FROM PARTS UNKNOWN...'MAD DOG' MICHAELS!
MY FIRST OPPONENT WAS 28-YEARS-OLD AND, LIKE ME, HAD ZERO IN-RING WRESTLING EXPERIENCE.

I WANTED A 'REAL' FIGHT, AND THAT'S EXACTLY WHAT I WAS GOING TO GET.

WE FOUGHT FOR WHAT SEEMED LIKE AN ETERNITY. PUNCHING. GOUGING. KICKING. STOMPING. WE BEAT EACH OTHER *BLACK AND BLUE*. TWO UNTRAINED WARRIORS IN AN UNBRIDLED WAR.

GET OUT HERE!
THEY'RE GONNA *KILL* EACH OTHER!

MY FIRST MATCH TOOK APPROXIMATELY *TWO MINUTES* BEFORE THE LOCKER ROOM CLEARED...

...AND AN *ARMY* OF WRESTLERS PILED INTO THE SQUARED CIRCLE...

...SEPARATING ME AND MAD DOG AND PREVENTING ANY PERMANENT INJURIES.

LADIES AND GENTLEMEN, WE HAVE A *DOUBLE* DISQUALIFICATION...

I WAS BEATEN AND BRUISED, BUT I LOVED IT...

...SIGNING MY FIRST AUTOGRAPHS...

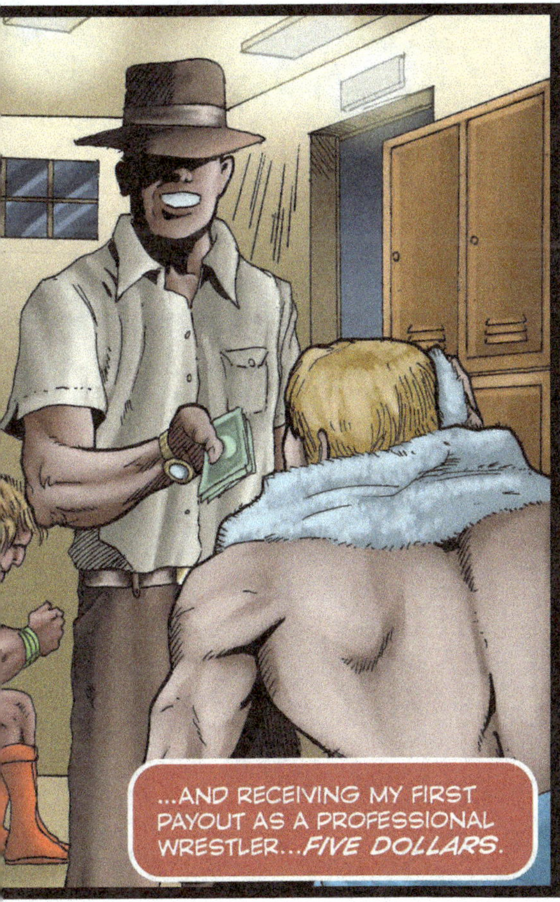
...AND RECEIVING MY FIRST PAYOUT AS A PROFESSIONAL WRESTLER...FIVE DOLLARS.

WELCOME TO THE SHOW, KID.
BOBBY FULTON HAD ARRIVED.

I WAS LIVING THE LIFE OF A TEEN-AGE *SUPERHERO*. ON WEEKDAYS, I WAS MILD-MANNERED HIGH SCHOOL STUDENT, *JIMMY HINES*.

BUT, ON THE WEEKENDS, I WAS PROFESSIONAL WRESTLING STAR, *BOBBY FULTON!*

BATTLING ALONGSIDE AND AGAINST CHILDHOOD IDOLS SUCH AS *'WILD BULL' CURRY* AND HIS SON, *'FLYING' FRED CURRY*.

WRESTLING HAD BECOME MY LIFE. WHILE MY FELLOW HIGH SCHOOL SENIORS WERE ATTENDING OUR HIGH SCHOOL GRADUATION...

...I WAS APPEARING FOR VINCE MCMAHON AND THE WWWF IN A TELEVISED MATCH AGAINST STEVE TRAVIS.

FOLLOWING MY GRADUATION FROM HIGH SCHOOL, AND AFTER A BRIEF STOP IN KENTUCKY, I TRAVELED TO NASHVILLE, TENNESSEE, WHERE I BEGAN TO WRESTLE FOR THE ***NWA MID-AMERICA*** PROMOTION OF ***NICK GULAS***.

JIMMY, THIS IS ***ERIC EMBRY***. I'M PAIRING THE TWO OF YOU TOGETHER. MEET YOUR BROTHER, ***DON FULTON***.

AND WAS PAIRED WITH ERIC EMBRY TO FORM THE 'BROTHER' TAG TEAM, ***THE FULTON BROTHERS***, CONSISTING OF ME AND EMBRY, WHO WOULD BE KNOWN AS 'DON FULTON'.

EMBRY AND I BEGAN TRAINING TOGETHER. KEY COMPONENTS TO A SUCCESSFUL TAG TEAM COMBINATION ARE TIMING AND COORDINATION.

...COMING TO THE RING AT THIS TIME... BOBBY AND DON FULTON... *THE FULTON BROTHERS!*

WE HAD A GOOD RUN IN NASHVILLE...

...BEFORE THE TEAM WAS DISSOLVED, AND I HEADED NORTH TO CANADA AND THE *STAMPEDE* WRESTLING PROMOTION OF THE LEGENDARY *STU HART*.

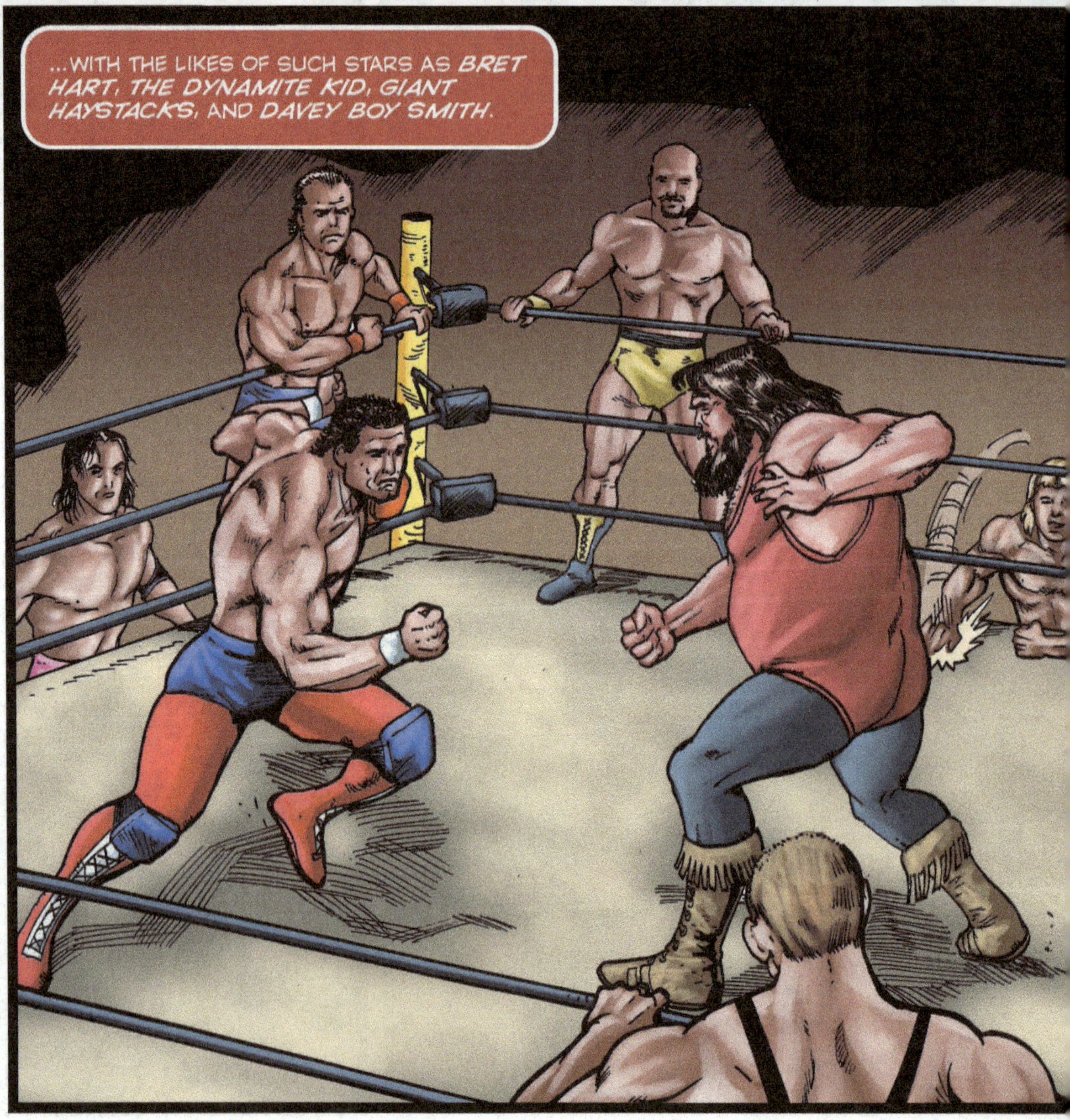

...WITH THE LIKES OF SUCH STARS AS *BRET HART, THE DYNAMITE KID, GIANT HAYSTACKS,* AND *DAVEY BOY SMITH.*

AND IT WAS IN CANADA THAT I FIRST BECAME A *CHAMPION*.
HEY, BOBBY! PUT ME IN A SMALL PACKAGE.
ARE YOU *SERIOUS*, LEN?
"CRAZY" DAVID PATTERSON AND *"THE GRAPPLER" LEN DENTON*, THE NORTH AMERICAN TAG TEAM CHAMPIONS.

YEAH. *SMALL PACKAGE* ME.

ONE...
TWO...
THREE!

CONGRATULATIONS, CHAMP!

PATTERSON AND DENTON HAD *LEFT* THE PROMOTION.

AND WITH THAT, *I* WAS THE NORTH AMERICAN TAG TEAM CHAMPIONS...

TO BE CONTINUED.

Bobby Fulton

The Developmental Years

Birth Name: James Hines
Born: October 4, 1960
Chillicothe, Ohio
Height: 5' 10"
Weight: 220 lbs
Career: 1977-2018

Art by Javier Lugo & Blake Wilkie

Determined from an early age to realize his dream of becoming a professional wrestler, James Hines began assisting with ring set-up and breakdown at Mid-West Wrestling Alliance shows at age 13. He learned the inner workings of the business and even benefited from some informal training by the local promotion's talent. By the tender age of 16, he decided on the ring name of Bobby Fulton and took part in his first real match at a Three Rivers Wrestling show in West Virginia.

Fulton's opponent in that first match was another first-time performer, Mad Dog Michaels, and the pair viciously fought to a double disqualification ended only when the rest of the card cleared the locker room to break them up. While still a teenager, he made appearances in Vince McMahon's World Wide Wrestling Federation (WWWF) and Nick Gulas' National Wrestling Alliance (NWA) Mid-America, teaming in the latter promotion with Eric Embry (under the ring name Don Fulton) as The Fulton Brothers.

After the dissolution of that pairing, Bobby moved on to Stampede Wrestling in Calgary, Alberta, where he trained with Stu Hart alongside Bret The Hitman Hart, The Dynamite Kid, and Davey Boy Smith. It was there that he won his first belt, and in bizarre fashion. He was approached at his home by the North American Tag Team Champions, Crazy David Patterson and The Grappler Len Denton and offered the chance to pin Denton via the small package maneuver. Surprised, Fulton nonetheless small-packaged Denton as Patterson counted three and left Fulton with the belts.

writer John E. Crowther
@crowman1971

artist Rich Perotta
@RichPerottaArt

colorist Blake Wilkie
@Tecracoon

flatter Amy Rachels

letterer Jessica Hinds
@Jessapalooza

editor/designer Kevin LaPorte
@kevinlaporte

THAT'S ME AND MY BROTHER FRANKIE. FRANKIE WAS ONE OF THE SMARTEST PEOPLE I KNEW...AND MY FIRST HERO.
HEY,, DORK!
FRANKIE WANKIE!
NERD!
BUT THE KIDS WERE CRUEL TO MY BROTHER. THEY TOOK PLEASURE IN TEASING AND TAUNTING HIM.
WHAT'S'A MATTER, BUTTERFINGERS? DID YOU DROP YOUR LITTLE BOOKS?

SO...SOMETIMES...I HAD TO BE THE HERO.
COME ON, TC. LET'S GO HOME.

I LOVE YOU, TC.
I LOVE YOU TOO, FRANKIE.
LOS ANGELES, CALIFORNIA – 1964.

MY NAME IS PATRICIA SUMMERLAND, BUT YOU CAN CALL ME "SUNNY". I WAS BORN IN SUNNY LOS ANGELES, CALIFORNIA, TO BIRTH PARENTS I WOULD NOT MEET FOR MANY YEARS.
I WAS RAISED BY MY AUNT AND UNCLE, MAMIE AND HENRY CHAMBERS, ALONG WITH MY COUSINS, TOMMY AND FRANKIE. THAT'S THEM TRYING TO SNEAK A PEEK AT THEIR NEW BABY SISTER.
HENRY WAS A POLICE OFFICER...
...WHO LATER RETIRED TO JOIN MAMIE AS AN AGENT WITH THE L.A. TIMES.

I LIVED A HAPPY CHILDHOOD, GROWING UP IN *LA CRESCENTA, CALIFORNIA*, SPENDING DAYS AT THE BEACH...
...ENJOYING TRADITIONAL HOLIDAYS, SUCH AS THANKSGIVING...
...CHRISTMAS...
...AND EASTER...
...AND ADMIRING MY BROTHERS, PARTICULARLY TOMMY, WHO BRAVELY SERVED HIS COUNTRY DURING THE VIETNAM WAR.

OLYMPIC AUDITORIUM. LOS ANGELES - 1969.
I WAS INTRODUCED TO PROFESSIONAL WRESTLING AT AN EARLY AGE, MY FIRST MEMORY BEING A FAMILY TRIP TO OLYMPIC AUDITORIUM IN DOWNTOWN LOS ANGELES WHEN I WAS FIVE YEARS OLD.

HENRY WAS CLOSE FRIENDS WITH MANY WRESTLERS AT THE TIME...
STAFF
...INCLUDING "CLASSY" FREDDIE BLASSIE...
...AND THE LEGENDARY DICK BEYER, A.K.A. THE DESTROYER.
HEY, PATRICIA. THOSE ARE SOME IMPRESSIVE BICEPS.
TRY IT ON, PATRICIA. I HAVE A FEELING YOU'RE DESTINED TO BE A FUTURE "DESTROYER".
I SUPPOSE WRESTLING WAS MY DESTINY.

GROWING UP, MOST PEOPLE WOULD DESCRIBE ME AS A TOMBOY.
I WAS AN ACCOMPLISHED ATHLETE, COMPETING IN VOLLEYBALL AND SOFTBALL...
...AND I WAS EXTREMELY COMPETITIVE, EVEN TAKING ON THE BOYS IN TRACK AND FIELD.
GO, TC!

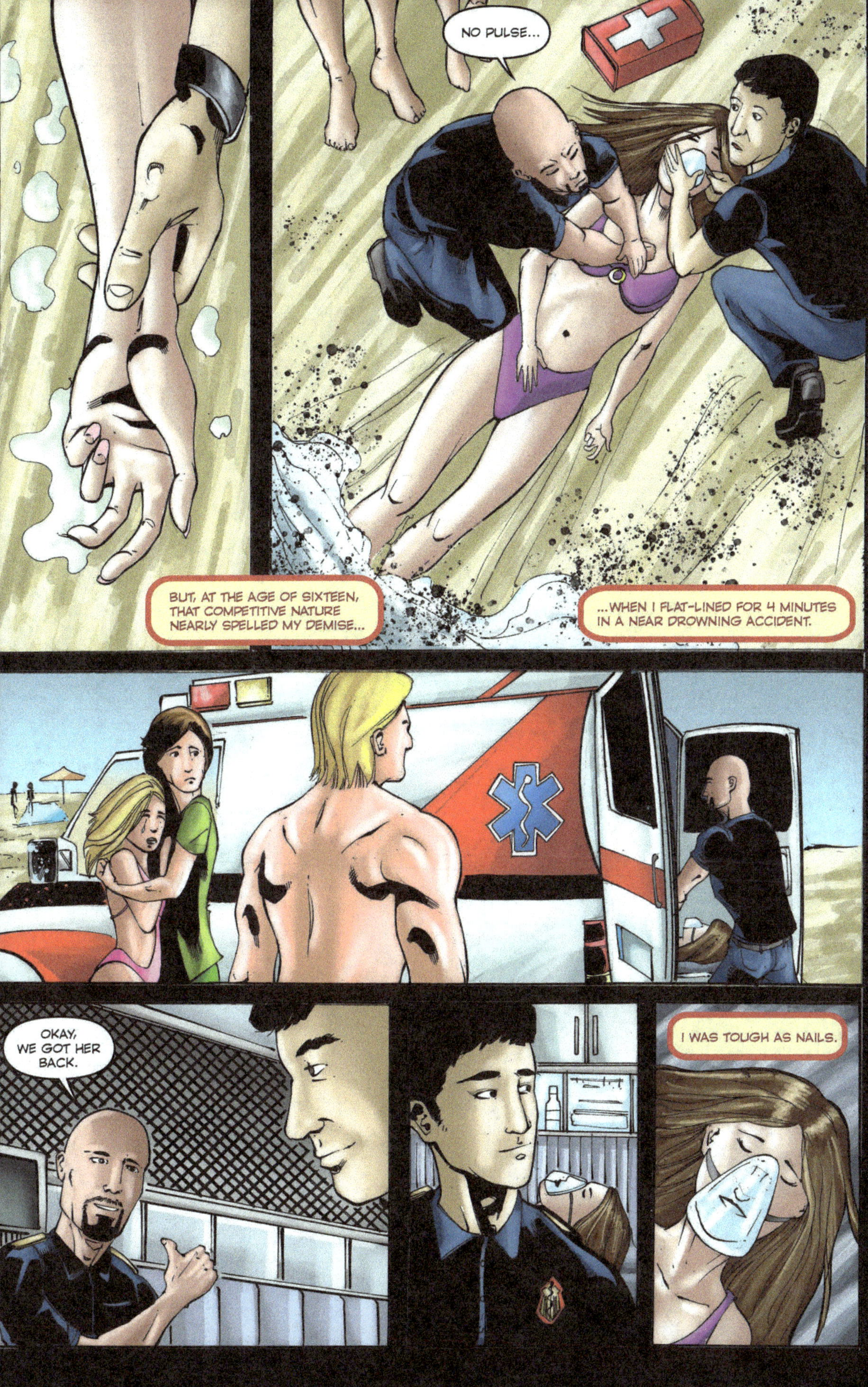
NO PULSE...
BUT, AT THE AGE OF SIXTEEN, THAT COMPETITIVE NATURE NEARLY SPELLED MY DEMISE...
...WHEN I FLAT-LINED FOR 4 MINUTES IN A NEAR DROWNING ACCIDENT.
OKAY, WE GOT HER BACK.
I WAS TOUGH AS NAILS.

AS A YOUNG TEENAGER, I BEGAN TO PURSUE ANOTHER PASSION...MODELING. I ATTENDED MODELING CLASSES TO LEARN PROPER ETIQUETTE AND RECEIVED PROFESSIONAL INSTRUCTION IN RUNWAY MODELING, PRINT MODELING, AND INTERVIEWING SKILLS, WHICH EVENTUALLY LED, AT THE AGE OF 15, TO A CONTRACT WITH *CATALINA SWIMWEAR*.

EARLY ADULTHOOD CAN BE A STRUGGLE FOR MANY, AND I WAS NO EXCEPTION.
IT WAS AS A YOUNG ADULT THAT I LEARNED THE TRUTH ABOUT MY BIRTH PARENTS.
FEELINGS OF MISTRUST LED ME TO A LIFE OF REBELLION. I ABANDONED MY ADOPTIVE PARENTS, TOOK THE SURNAME "SUMMERLAND", AND TACKLED THE LOS ANGELES PARTY SCENE.
I RUBBED ELBOWS WITH CELEBRITIES... LIVING LIFE TO ITS FULLEST...BUT I WAS STILL SEARCHING FOR MY DESTINY.

IT WAS A SATURDAY MORNING IN 1986 WHEN, WHILE WATCHING AN EPISODE OF *G.L.O.W. (THE GORGEOUS LADIES OF WRESTLING)* WITH HENRY, THE PATH TO MY DESTINY RETURNED.
PATRICIA, WILL YOU LOOK AT THESE GIRLS! *YOU* COULD DO THIS.
G.L.O.W.
ARE YOU *CRAZY?* THEY'D KILL ME.
I'M SERIOUS. *YOU* CAN DO THIS. *YOU'RE* AN ATHLETE.
203
555-0819
NOW
ACCEPTING AUDITIONS

I TOOK A CHANCE, SUBMITTED MY APPLICATION...AND GUESS WHO CALLED BACK. THAT'S RIGHT...
TO Fabulous LAS VEGAS NEVADA
...I WAS ON MY WAY TO VEGAS.
I TRAINED FOR SIX WEEKS, COMPETING WITH 400 WOMEN FOR 36 AVAILABLE SPOTS ON THE G.L.O.W. ROSTER.
AFTER THE FINAL CUT, SHOW CREATOR AND DIRECTOR, MATT CIMBER, CONGRATULATED US ON OUR ACHIEVEMENT.
CONGRATULATIONS, LADIES! YOU'VE MADE IT THIS FAR...THE FINAL 36... BUT, NOW, YOUR WORK REALLY BEGINS.
I'M SURE YOU KNOW THESE TWO WOMEN STANDING BESIDE ME...COLONEL NINOTCHKA AND DEBBIE DEBUTANTE. LADIES, MEET YOUR TRAINERS.

I TRAINED FOR THREE ADDITIONAL MONTHS...LEARNING HOLDS, PERFECTING MY TIMING, AND STRENGTHENING MY SKILLS ON THE MICROPHONE.

MY IN-RING SKILLS HONED, I MET WITH *MATT CIMBER* AND *G.L.O.W.* WRITER, *STEVE BLANCE*, TO DETERMINE THE CHARACTER I WOULD PORTRAY FOR THE SHOW.
PATRICIA, AS YOU KNOW, *CALIFORNIA DOLL* WAS A POPULAR CHARACTER FOR US, BUT SHE'S NO LONGER HERE.
I ENVISION YOU AS A "NEW" VERSION OF *CALIFORNIA DOLL*. A VERSION BASED ON MY EX-WIFE, *JANE MANSFIELD*. I WANT YOU TO STUDY MANSFIELD. LEARN HER MANNERISMS.
YOU'RE FROM SUNNY *CALIFORNIA*, SO WE'LL CALL YOU *"SUNNY THE CALIFORNIA GIRL"*. YOUR FIRST LIVE MATCH IS IN TWO WEEKS. BE READY!
YOU BETTER BELIEVE I'LL BE READY!

SHOWBOAT CASINO, LAUGHLIN, NEVADA – 1987.
THE BIG NIGHT HAD ARRIVED...MY FIRST LIVE WRESTLING EVENT, A TAG TEAM MATCH BEFORE A PACKED CROWD.
MY TAG TEAM PARTNER THAT NIGHT WAS G.L.O.W. VETERAN, CHEYENNE CHER.
THAT NIGHT, WE FACED...
...AND THEIR OPPONENTS... THE TEAM OF HOLLYWOOD AND VINE!
DING
DING
DING

IT WAS A WELL-FOUGHT MATCH...
...BUT OUR OPPONENTS, AS USUAL, EMPLOYED THEIR UNDERHANDED TACTICS AND STOLE THE VICTORY.

I FACED MANY GIRLS ON THE G.L.O.W. ROSTER THAT YEAR, BUT MY MOST DIFFICULT OPPONENT, BY FAR, WAS THE INTIMIDATING POWERHOUSE AND PRACTITIONER OF THE VOODOO ARTS...BIG BAD MAMA.
I'M NOT AFRAID OF YOU, BIG BAD MAMA!
SUNNY IS BRAVE, BUT IT APPEARS THAT BIG BAD MAMA HAS SPRINKLED SUNNY WITH VOODOO DUST!
I HAD PREPARED TO FACE THE MASSIVE STRENGTH OF BIG BAD MAMA, BUT I WAS NOT PREPARED TO DO BATTLE WITH HER VOODOO POWERS AND THE MANIPULATION OF HER MAGICAL VOODOO DOLL.

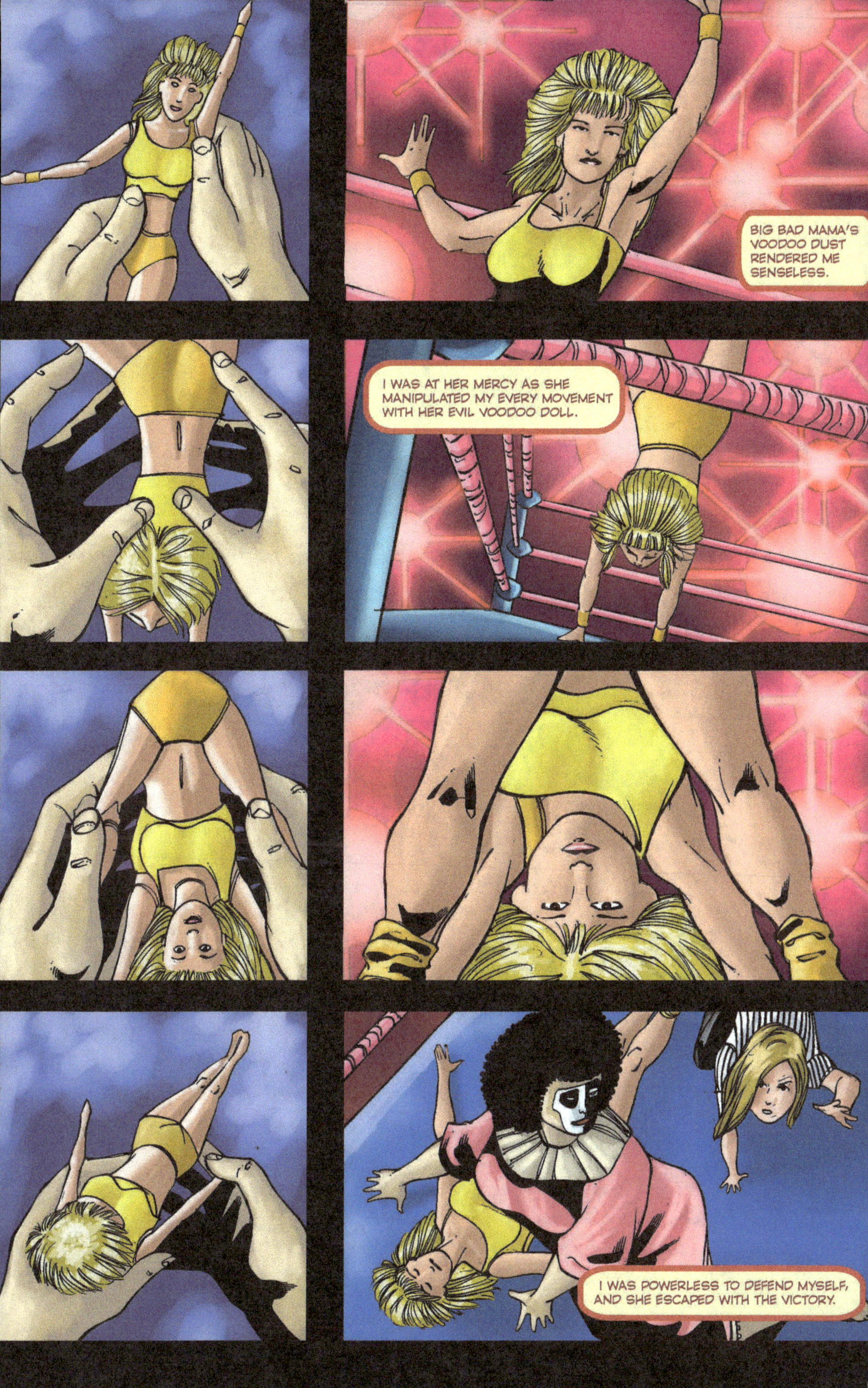
BIG BAD MAMA'S VOODOO DUST RENDERED ME SENSELESS.
I WAS AT HER MERCY AS SHE MANIPULATED MY EVERY MOVEMENT WITH HER EVIL VOODOO DOLL.
I WAS POWERLESS TO DEFEND MYSELF, AND SHE ESCAPED WITH THE VICTORY.

AS THE YEAR 1988 PROGRESSED, I CONTINUED TO TRAIN AND COMPETE FOR G.L.O.W., BUT I WAS TORN. WHILE I COMPETED AS SUNNY THE CALIFORNIA GIRL, MY FATHER, *HENRY*, WAS DEATHLY ILL AT HOME.

THOUGHTS OF MY FATHER BEGAN TO AFFECT ME IN THE RING.
COME ON, SUNNY. PAY ATTENTION.
SUNNY, GET OVER HERE.
WHAT'S THE PROBLEM, SUNNY? IT'S YOUR DAD, ISN'T IT?
IT'S NOTHING. I'LL BE ALL RIGHT.
YOU'VE GOT TO GET YOUR MIND STRAIGHT, OR YOU'RE GOING TO GET HURT IN THE RING. GO SEE YOUR DAD. WE'LL BE HERE WHEN YOU GET BACK.
I GRABBED MY GEAR AND LEFT. SUNNY WOULD HAVE TO WAIT. PATRICIA WAS NEEDED AT HOME.

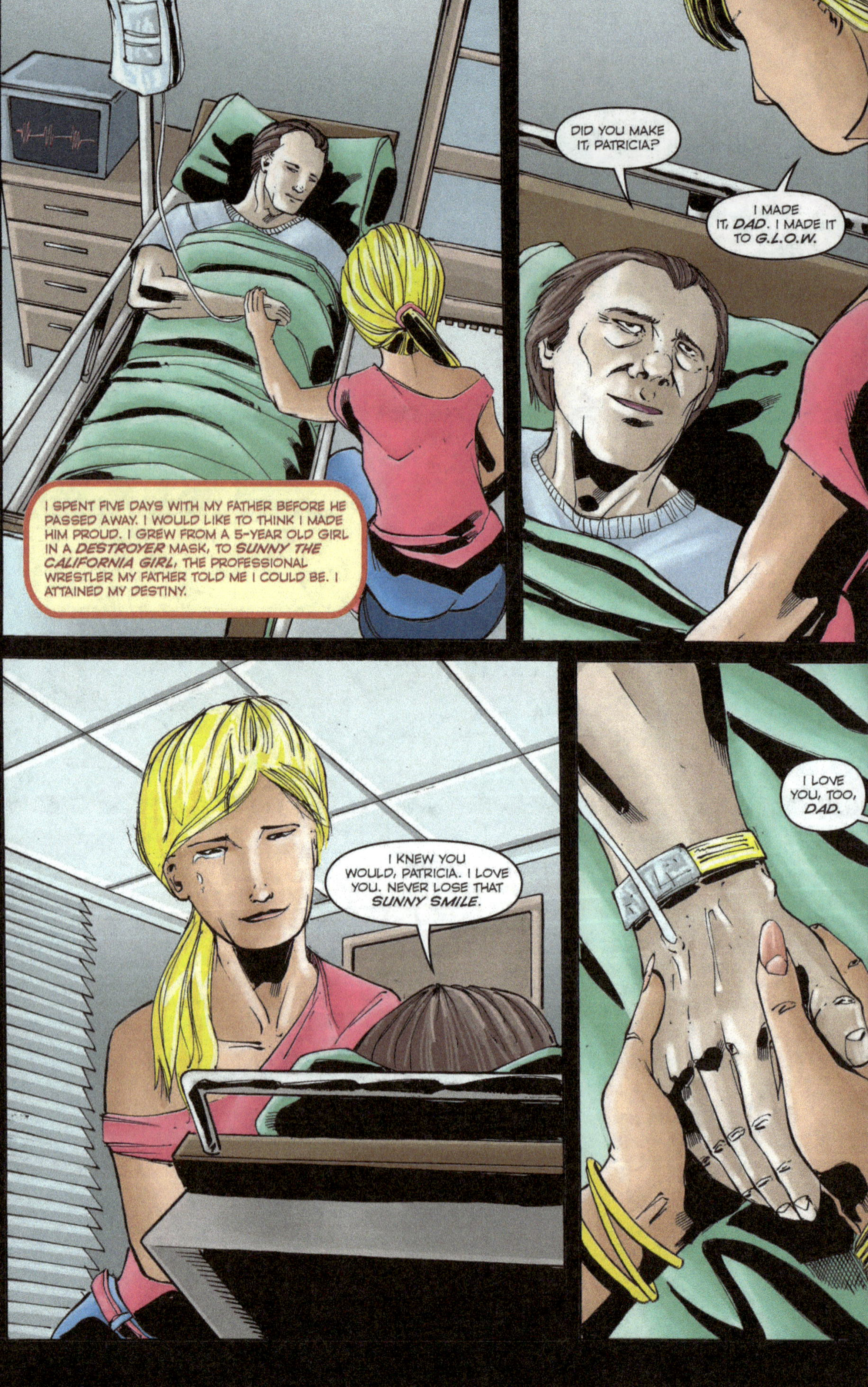
I SPENT FIVE DAYS WITH MY FATHER BEFORE HE PASSED AWAY. I WOULD LIKE TO THINK I MADE HIM PROUD. I GREW FROM A 5-YEAR OLD GIRL IN A *DESTROYER* MASK, TO *SUNNY THE CALIFORNIA GIRL*, THE PROFESSIONAL WRESTLER MY FATHER TOLD ME I COULD BE. I ATTAINED MY DESTINY.
DID YOU MAKE IT, PATRICIA?
I MADE IT, *DAD*. I MADE IT TO *G.L.O.W.*
I KNEW YOU WOULD, PATRICIA. I LOVE YOU. NEVER LOSE THAT *SUNNY SMILE*.
I LOVE YOU, TOO, *DAD*.

IMMEDIATELY FOLLOWING THE PASSING OF MY FATHER, I ATTEMPTED TO RETURN TO *G.L.O.W.*, BUT THE ORGANIZATION HAD FOLDED. *G.L.O.W.* AS A WRESTLING ENTITY WAS NO MORE.
A GOOD PORTION OF THE ROSTER STILL UNITES, AND YOU CAN FIND US ANNUALLY ON OUR *AFTERGLOW* FAN CRUISE. IN 2017, THE *G.L.O.W.* ROSTER WAS HONORED BY THE CAULIFLOWER ALLEY CLUB FOR OUR CONTRIBUTIONS TO THE WRESTLING INDUSTRY, AND I WAS PRESENTED WITH A *CHAMPIONSHIP* BELT.
SUNNY WAS PUT ON HOLD THAT DAY IN 1989, BUT SHE'S NEVER FAR AWAY. KEEP SMILING THOSE *SUNNY* SMILES...AND SHE JUST MIGHT RETURN.

Sunny

The California Girl

Real Name: Patricia Summerland
Born: Nov. 12, 1966 Los Angeles, CA
Height: 5' 10"
Career: 1986-Present

Patricia Summerland was raised by an aunt and uncle in La Crescenta, California, and was introduced to professional wrestling in childhood. Her uncle knew some of the Southern California workers at the time, allowing Patricia the opportunity to meet Classy Freddie Blassie and Dick the Destroyer while just a little girl. She was a competitive athlete through high school, participating in volleyball, softball, and track and field, and she also took professional modeling classes as a teenager.

At just fifteen years old, she inked a contract with Catalina Swimwear and also modeled for Jordache Jeans. In 1986, Patricia discovered the Gorgeous Ladies of Wrestling (G.L.O.W.) in syndication on local television, and she answered an ad to audition. The novel promotion accepted her application, and she spent six weeks training in Las Vegas, competing with hundreds of other women for just thirty-six available spots. She made the cut, replacing the California Doll character no longer with the company with an updated version, Sunny the California Girl, also partially based on the persona of Hollywood bombshell, Jane Mansfield.

In her first live wrestling match, Sunny teamed with Cheyenne Cher to face the foremost heel tag team in G.L.O.W., Hollywood and Vine, recording a loss to the veteran duo. She went on to memorable matches with Big Bad Mama and her voodoo gimmick, as well as with Beastie, before leaving G.L.O.W. to care for her ailing uncle. Unfortunately, the promotion folded before her return, but she enjoyed a successful career modeling NFL apparel and appearing in a Playboy shoot with KISS.

Jake Hager

The Developmental Years

Ring Name:	Jack Swagger
Born:	March 24, 1982
	Fargo, ND
Spouse:	Catalina (m. 2010)
Height:	6' 7"
Weight:	275 lbs
Career:	2006-Present

Jake Hager hails from a family of successful amateur wrestlers, including his cousin, Ryan Kringlie, who won the 1991 Junior National Championship in Greco-Roman wrestling while competing for Oregon State University and was later inducted into the North Dakota Wrestling Hall of Fame.

Hager himself began competing at Perry (Oklahoma) High School, a program that had won 38 team state championships.

He won the Oklahoma State Championship in the 215-pound class in his junior and senior years, and, in 2000, he was invited to the Junior National Wrestling Team. His successes on the mat earned him a wrestling scholarship to The University of Oklahoma, a program with seven National Championships in the sport. He would also play defensive tackle for the Sooners and was an Academic All-American.

In 2005, at a University of Oklahoma event, his football teammate, Dusty Dvoracek, introduced him to Jim Ross and Gerry Brisco, both then executives with World Wrestling Entertainment (WWE), and Ross offered to arrange a tryout after Hager's graduation. In the meantime, Hager qualified for both the 2005 and 2006 NCAA Division I Wrestling Championships and twice helped the Sooners to third-place finishes. He earned a degree in finance but was offered a WWE contract the same day he was to begin his first job. He trained with Deep South Wrestling under Bill DeMott and Dr. Death Steve Williams before joining Florida Championship Wrestling and claiming the Florida Heavyweight Championship in a match against Ted DiBiase, Jr.

writer John E. Crowther
@crowman1971

artist/letterer Alan McMillian
@Alan_McMillian

colorist Andrew Pate
@Andrew_Pate

editor/designer Kevin LaPorte
@kevinlaporte

WE, THE PEOPLE!
WE, THE PEOPLE!
WE, THE PEOPLE!
WE, THE PEOPLE!

THIS IS MY STORY. THE STORY OF JAKE HAGER....FORMERLY KNOWN AS "JACK SWAGGER".

I WAS BORN ON MARCH 24, 1982, IN FARGO, NORTH DAKOTA.
AT THE AGE OF FOUR, WE PACKED OUR BELONGINGS AND LEFT THE COLD OF FARGO...
... FOR PERRY, OKLAHOMA....
DITCH WITCH
...HOME OF THE DITCH WITCH FACTORY...
...AND WRESTLING.

MY OLDER COUSINS, SUCH AS RYAN KRINGLIE, WERE SELECTED FOR THE 1991 ASICS DREAM TEAM.
I CAUGHT THE BUG EARLY, SOAKING UP THE MATCHES AND STUDYING TECHNIQUES.
KRINGLIE WOULD GO ON TO COMPETE COLLEGIATELY AT OREGON STATE, WIN THE 1991 JUNIOR NATIONAL CHAMPIONSHIP IN GRECO-ROMAN WRESTLING, AND BE INDUCTED INTO THE NORTH DAKOTA WRESTLING HALL OF FAME .
THANKS FOR COMIN' OUT, JAKE!
I SUPPOSE YOU COULD SAY WRESTLING WAS IN MY BLOOD.

PERRY
HIGH
SCHOOL
MY LOVE AND DEVOTION FOR WRESTLING GREW DURING MY HIGH SCHOOL YEARS.
PERRY HIGH SCHOOL WAS A POWERHOUSE IN WRESTLING, WINNING MORE STATE CHAMPIONSHIPS THAN ANY OTHER HIGH SCHOOL IN THE NATION.
38 STATE CHAMPIONSHIPS AS A TEAM...
...AND OVER 150 INDIVIDUAL STATE CHAMPIONS.

PERRY WAS A HUB OF AMATEUR WRESTLING AND WHO BETTER TO DEFINE WRESTLING THAN PERRY'S VERY OWN DANNY HODGE, WHOSE GRANDSON WAS A TEAMMATE OF MINE AT PERRY HIGH.
LOOK CLOSELY BOYS.
SKRUNCH!
HODGE WAS KNOWN, NOT ONLY FOR HIS WRESTLING ENDEAVORS, BUT ALSO FOR A FEAT OF STRENGTH HE WOULD PERFORM FOR RAPT AUDIENCES.

HODGE WAS AN ACCOMPLISHED AMATEUR WRESTLER, WINNING THREE NCAA CHAMPIONSHIPS, WHILE ATTENDING THE UNIVERSITY OF OKLAHOMA...
...AND A SILVER MEDAL AT THE 1956 OLYMPICS IN MELBOURNE, AUSTRALIA.
HE WAS A SUCCESSFUL BOXER, WINNING THE 1958 CHICAGO GOLDEN GLOVES CHAMPIONSHIP, AND SPORTING A PROFESSIONAL RECORD OF 8-2.
AND, AS A PROFESSIONAL WRESTLER, HE WAS A 5-TIME UNITED STATES TAG TEAM CHAMPION AND 7-TIME NWA JUNIOR HEAVYWEIGHT CHAMPION. WITHOUT A DOUBT, HE WAS A LEGEND IN PERRY.

I WAS A STANDOUT AND A LEADER IN HIGH SCHOOL, SERVING AS CLASS PRESIDENT MY SOPHOMORE AND JUNIOR YEARS...
MAROON 72
...AND DOMINANT ON THE FOOTBALL FIELD...
LAPORTE
...BOTH ON THE OFFENSIVE...
HAGER 72
...AND THE DEFENSIVE LINE.
MAROON

BUT WRESTLING WAS MY TRUE LOVE. BY 1999, I WAS THE SECOND-RANKED 215 POUNDER IN THE NATION, AS DETERMINED BY WRESTLING USA...
Wrestling

...AND, AFTER A RUNNER-UP FINISH MY SOPHOMORE YEAR, I WON THE STATE CHAMPIONSHIP IN THE 215-POUND CLASS BOTH MY JUNIOR AND SENIOR YEARS, LEADING TO MY INCLUSION ON THE JUNIOR NATIONAL WRESTLING TEAM IN THE SUMMER OF 2000.

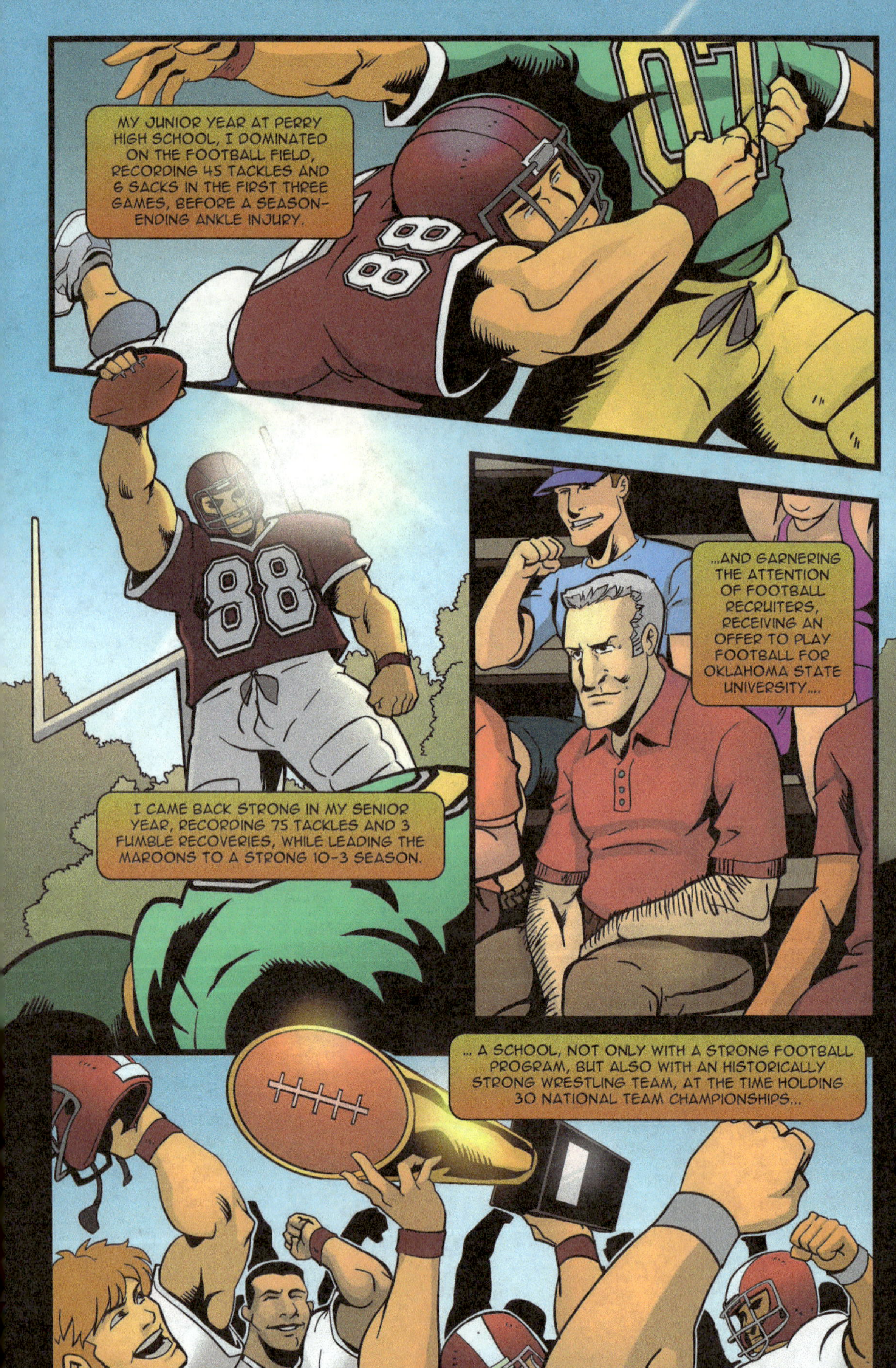
MY JUNIOR YEAR AT PERRY HIGH SCHOOL, I DOMINATED ON THE FOOTBALL FIELD, RECORDING 45 TACKLES AND 6 SACKS IN THE FIRST THREE GAMES, BEFORE A SEASON-ENDING ANKLE INJURY.
I CAME BACK STRONG IN MY SENIOR YEAR, RECORDING 75 TACKLES AND 3 FUMBLE RECOVERIES, WHILE LEADING THE MAROONS TO A STRONG 10-3 SEASON.
...AND GARNERING THE ATTENTION OF FOOTBALL RECRUITERS, RECEIVING AN OFFER TO PLAY FOOTBALL FOR OKLAHOMA STATE UNIVERSITY....
... A SCHOOL, NOT ONLY WITH A STRONG FOOTBALL PROGRAM, BUT ALSO WITH AN HISTORICALLY STRONG WRESTLING TEAM, AT THE TIME HOLDING 30 NATIONAL TEAM CHAMPIONSHIPS...

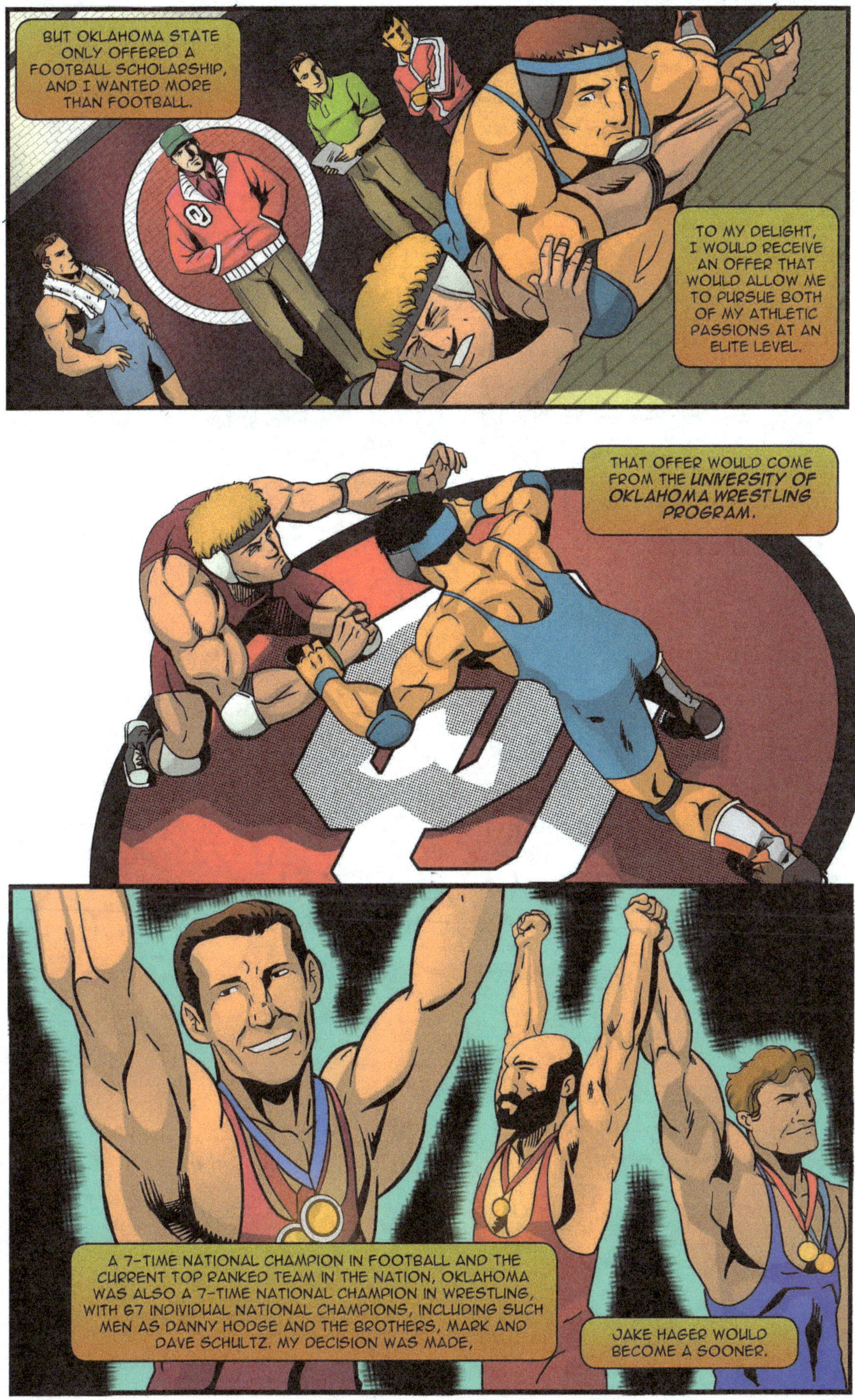

THAT OFFER WOULD COME FROM THE ***UNIVERSITY OF OKLAHOMA WRESTLING PROGRAM.***

A 7-TIME NATIONAL CHAMPION IN FOOTBALL AND THE CURRENT TOP RANKED TEAM IN THE NATION, OKLAHOMA WAS ALSO A 7-TIME NATIONAL CHAMPION IN WRESTLING, WITH 67 INDIVIDUAL NATIONAL CHAMPIONS, INCLUDING SUCH MEN AS DANNY HODGE AND THE BROTHERS, MARK AND DAVE SCHULTZ. MY DECISION WAS MADE,

JAKE HAGER WOULD BECOME A SOONER.

THE UNIVERSITY OF OKLAHOMA, LOCATED IN NORMAN, WAS FOUNDED IN 1850, AND IS ONE OF THE TOP PUBLIC UNIVERSITIES IN THE UNITED STATES,
SOONER
OKLAHOMA
SOONER
WITH A PROUD TRADITION, NOT ONLY IN ACADEMICS, BUT ALSO IN ATHLETICS.
IN TOTAL, THE UNIVERSITY HAS CLAIMED 36 NATIONAL CHAMPIONSHIPS ACROSS A VARIETY OF SPORTS, INCLUDING BASEBALL, SOFTBALL, GYMNASTICS, FOOTBALL, AND WRESTLING. IT'S SAFE TO SAY I WAS AMONG CHAMPIONS.

I MADE THE MOST OF WHAT THIS GREAT UNIVERSITY HAD TO OFFER, QUALIFYING AS AN ACADEMIC ALL-AMERICAN. ON THE FOOTBALL FIELD,

HAGER
33
I PLAYED BEFORE HOME CROWDS AT OKLAHOMA MEMORIAL STADIUM IN EXCESS OF 80,000 SCREAMING FANS....

..AND, FOR MY FRESHMAN YEAR, MADE MY PRESENCE FELT AS A SECOND STRING DEFENSIVE TACKLE BEHIND FUTURE NFL PLAYERS:

GREAT GAME, JAKE!
...TOMMIE HARRIS AND DUSTY DVORACEK.

I LOVED THE GAME OF FOOTBALL, BUT IT WAS IN THE GYM, ON THE MAT, IN THE ULTIMATE INDIVIDUAL SPORT, PITTING ONE MAN AGAINST ANOTHER...WRESTLING...
...THAT I FELT MOST AT HOME.
DUSTY, HAVE YOU GOT A MINUTE?
OF COURSE, JAKE. WHAT'S ON YOUR MIND.
I DON'T FEEL I'M AT MY TOP WRESTLING FORM WHEN I AM IN FOOTBALL CONDITION.
I LOVE BOTH SPORTS BUT MY HEART IS WITH WRESTLING.
LET ME ASK YOU A QUESTION, JAKE: DO YOU SEE YOURSELF IN THE NFL?
NO.
THEN LET IT GO. WITH YOUR TALENT, IF YOU CONCENTRATE ON WRESTLING, YOU'LL BE COMPETING FOR NATIONAL CHAMPIONSHIPS.
WITH MY THOUGHTS CONFIRMED, I STEPPED AWAY FROM FOOTBALL AND DEDICATED MY ATHLETIC ENDEAVORS TO THE SPORT OF WRESTLING.

AT AN EVENT HOSTED BY THE UNIVERSITY OF OKLAHOMA IN 2005, MY FORMER FOOTBALL TEAMMATE, DUSTY DVORACEK, INTRODUCED ME TO A PAIR OF MEN WHO WOULD LAY THE GROUNDWORK FOR MY FUTURE AS A PROFESSIONAL WRESTLER...

...JIM ROSS AND GERRY BRISCO.
JIM ROSS WAS A SOONER ALUMNUS AND HAD BEEN INVOLVED WITH PROFESSIONAL WRESTLING SINCE THE 1970S WHEN, FRESH OUT OF COLLEGE, HE BEGAN COMMENTATING FOR THE NWA TRI-STATE PROMOTION.

BRISCO WAS A WRESTLING LEGEND. AFTER WRESTLING AS AN AMATEUR AT OKLAHOMA STATE, HE DEBUTED AS A PROFESSIONAL IN 1969 AS A TAG TEAM PARTNER WITH HIS BROTHER, JACK BRISCO, AND WOULD GO ON TO AMASS NUMEROUS TITLES.

BOTH MEN WERE NOW EXECUTIVES WITH THE WWE, ROSS AS HEAD OF TALENT RELATIONS.
IF YOU LOVE WRESTLING, THERE'S NO NEED TO STOP.
WHEN YOU GRADUATE, GIVE ME A CALL. I'LL ARRANGE A TRYOUT. WITH YOUR LOOKS, SIZE, AND ABILITY, YOU COULD BE A STAR IN THIS BUSINESS, JAKE.
I APPRECIATE THAT, MR. ROSS.

2005, MY JUNIOR YEAR, I WAS NOW ABLE TO FOCUS SOLELY ON WRESTLING.

I STEPPED UP MY TRAINING...

...AND QUALIFIED FOR THE 2005 NCAA DIVISION I WRESTLING CHAMPIONSHIPS IN ST. LOUIS, MISSOURI.

I WON MY FIRST ROUND MATCH...

...BUT DROPPED MY SECOND ROUND MATCH AGAINST THE UNIVERSITY OF PENNSYLVANIA'S MATT FEAST

WHILE I FAILED TO PLACE IN THE TOURNAMENT, I DID SUCCEED IN HELPING THE TEAM TO A THIRD PLACE FINISH.

ALL-AMERICAN
MY SENIOR YEAR, I CAME BACK STRONGER, DEFEATING FUTURE NATIONAL CHAMPION DUSTIN FOX, EARNING ALL-AMERICAN STATUS AND SETTING THE UNIVERSITY OF OKLAHOMA RECORD FOR PINS IN A SEASON, WITH 30.

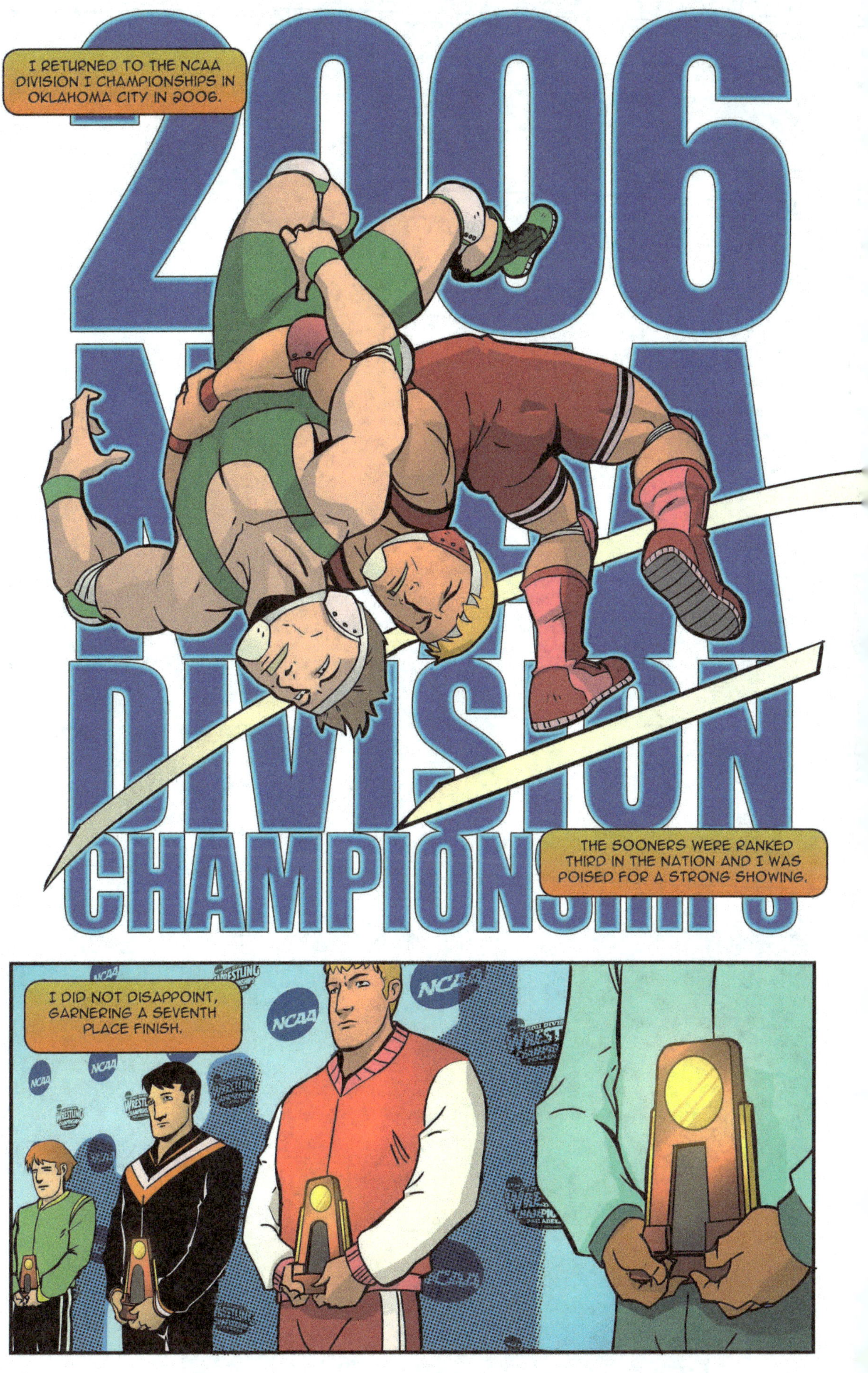

I RETURNED TO THE NCAA DIVISION I CHAMPIONSHIPS IN OKLAHOMA CITY IN 2006.

THE SOONERS WERE RANKED THIRD IN THE NATION AND I WAS POISED FOR A STRONG SHOWING.

I GRADUATED THAT YEAR WITH A BACHELOR'S DEGREE IN FINANCE...
...AND ACCEPTED A POSITION WITH A FIRM IN DALLAS, TEXAS.
BUT THE DAY I WAS TO BEGIN MY JOB IN DALLAS, I WAS OFFERED A CONTRACT WITH THE WWE
MY CAREER HAD TAKEN A DECIDEDLY DIFFERENT TURN.

IN MAY 2006, AS PROMISED, JIM ROSS ARRANGED A TRYOUT WITH WWE AFFILIATE, DEEP SOUTH WRESTLING, AND THEIR TRAINERS, BILL DEMOTT AND "DR. DEATH" STEVE WILLIAMS.
BOTH DEMOTT AND WILLIAMS WERE VETERANS, HAVING A COMBINED 38 YEARS IN THE INDUSTRY.
DEMOTT WAS KNOWN FOR HIS HARDCORE WRESTLING STYLE, WHICH HE INCORPORATED THROUGHOUT HIS YEARS IN ECW, WCW, AND WWE.
"DR. DEATH" WAS AN OKLAHOMA LEGEND. AN ALL-AMERICAN IN BOTH WRESTLING AND FOOTBALL AT THE UNIVERSITY OF OKLAHOMA, HE WENT ON TO A STORIED CAREER AS A PROFESSIONAL WRESTLER, WINNING MULTIPLE CHAMPIONSHIPS IN THE NWA, WCW, ECW, NJPW, AND WWE.
I WAS LEARNING FROM THE BEST.

IN SEPTEMBER OF THAT YEAR, I MADE MY PROFESSIONAL WRESTLING IN-RING DEBUT FOR DEPP SOUTH IN A DARK MATCH AGAINST ANTONIO MESTRE.
HIS OPPONENT, HAILING FROM PERRY, OKLAHOMA....
JAKE HAGER!
IN A WELL-ORCHESTRATED MATCH, I SECURED THE PIN FALL AND NOTCHED MY FIRST VICTORY AS A PROFESSIONAL.

IN AUGUST 2007, I LEFT DEEP SOUTH FOR ANOTHER WWE AFFILIATE....FLORIDA CHAMPIONSHIP WRESTLING, AND, AFTER ESTABLISHING MYSELF AS A HEEL IN THE ORGANIZATION, I WAS ENTERED INTO A 23-MAN BATTLE ROYAL TO DETERMINE THE FCW FLORIDA HEAVYWEIGHT CHAMPION.
IT WAS A FREE-FOR-ALL MATCH. EVERY MAN FOR HIMSELF. A WRESTLER IS ELIMINATED WHEN HE IS TOSSED OVER THE TOP ROPE AND BOTH FEET TOUCH THE FLOOR.
THE LAST TWO WRESTERS IN THE RING WOULD FACE EACH OTHER FOR THE FLORIDA HEAVYWEIGHT CHAMPIONSHIP. I WAS DETERMINED TO MAKE IT TO THE CHAMPIONSHIP MATCH.

IN THE END, ONLY TWO MEN WERE LEFT STANDING...

ME AND TED DIBIASE, JR., THE SON AND NAMESAKE OF WWE LEGEND "MILLION DOLLAR MAN" TED DIBIASE.

DIBIASE AND I BATTLED TOOTH AND NAIL. TWO YOUNG WRESTLERS FIGHTING IT OUT FOR THE TOP PRIZE IN FLORIDA CHAMPIONSHIP WRESTLING.
IN THE END, I PREVAILED, AND WALKED AWAY THE FIRST EVER FCW FLORIDA HEAVYWEIGHT CHAMPION.

I WASN'T SATISFIED WITH THE FLORIDA HEAVYWEIGHT CHAMPIONSHIP, NOT WITH ANOTHER HEAVYWEIGHT CHAMPIONSHIP BELT IN FCW...
...THE SOUTHERN HEAVYWEIGHT CHAMPIONSHIP HELD BY "HANDSOME" HEATH MILLER, KNOWN TODAY AS HEATH SLATER.
I WAS UNDEFEATED IN FCW AND HEADED TO THE RING. BOTH TITLES ON THE LINE. ONE OF US WOULD BECOME THE UNDISPUTED FCW HEAVYWEIGHT CHAMPION.

MILLER FOUGHT HARD, BUT HE COULDN'T OVERCOME MY UNDEFEATED RECORD.
IN THE END, HE WAS NO MATCH FOR THE STRENGTH, STAMINA, AND ATHLETICISM OF THE ALL AMERICAN FROM OKLAHOMA.
I LEFT WITH BOTH TITLES. I WAS THE UNDISPUTED FCW HEAVYWEIGHT CHAMPION. MY LIFE AS A CHAMPION HAD BEGUN.
TO BE CONTINUED...

The Comic Book Encyclopedia of Pro Wrestling

ACKNOWLEDGEMENTS

PREMIER BACKERS

JOE R. CHAVARRIA
CLAYTON FISHER
LUKE HELMER
SHAWN HUNT
JOHN MILLER
PETER MURRIETA
AARON PULEY
RATED R WRESTLING
OSCAR SHARPE
JAMYLEE SMITH

THANK YOU TO THE LEGENDS OF THE SQUARED CIRCLE WHO SHARED THEIR STORIES WITH US:

JOSIP PERUZOVIC
B. BRIAN BLAIR
LANNY POFFO
JIM BRUNZELL
JIM DUGGAN
JIMMY HINES
BRUNO SAMMARTINO
RICKY MORTON
JAKE HAGER
PATRICIA SUMMERLAND

The Comic Book ENCYCLOPEDIA of Pro Wrestling

A FEW OF OUR CREATORS

JOHN CROWTHER

JOHN IS A FREELANCE COMIC BOOK WRITER, HAVING CREATED AND WRITTEN FOR SEVERAL PUBLISHERS, INCLUDING HEAVY METAL MAGAZINE, ANTARCTIC PRESS, UNLIKELY HEROES STUDIOS, TIN SKY MEDIA, AND CALIBER COMICS. HE AUTHORED EACH INSTALLMENT OF THE GROWING LINE OF AUTHORIZED WRESTLING COMICS PUBLISHED BY SQUARED CIRCLE COMICS, INCLUDING NIKOLAI, BRUNO SAMMARTINO, HACKSAW JIM DUGGAN, THE GENIUS LANNY POFFO, AND THE SOULMAN ROCKY JOHNSON.

KEVIN LaPORTE

KEVIN IS A WRITER, PUBLISHER AND EDITOR OF INDIE COMICS, HEADQUARTERED IN FAIRHOPE, ALABAMA. WITH HIS PARTNER, AMANDA RACHELS, HE FOUNDED INVERSE PRESS AND HAS SINCE PRODUCED A BURGEONING CATALOGUE OF COMICS STEEPED IN THE WEIRD AND HORRIFIC, WITH AN UNDERLYING DARK HUMOR.

RICH PEROTTA

STARTING AS AN INTERN FOR THE X-MEN OFFICE, RICH SOON BECAME A STAFF ARTIST AND THEN A FREELANCE INKER FOR MARVEL WITH A DASH OF DARK HORSE AND CRUSADE ENTERTAINMENT THROWN IN FOR GOOD MEASURE. RICH INKED FOR MARVEL FOR ROUGHLY TEN YEARS BEFORE TAKING A BREAK FROM COMICS. HE LATER RE-ENTERED THE COMIC INDUSTRY WORKING FOR DC COMICS, INKING TITLES BOOSTER GOLD AND THE RAY LIMITED SERIES. RICH IS NOW PENCILLING INDEPENDENT TITLES FOR SOURCE POINT PRESS, INVERSE PRESS, AND SQUARED CIRCLE COMICS.

DELL BARRAS

DELL IS A LEGEND IN THE COMIC BOOK INDUSTRY, WORKING FOR DC COMICS, MARVEL, AND ANTARCTIC PRESS ON MANY TITLES, INCLUDING CONAN THE BARBARIAN, THE AMAZING SPIDER MAN, BLUE BEETLE AND DEATH'S HEAD II. HE ALSO WORKED EXTENSIVELY AS A STORYBOARD ARTIST FOR WARNER BROTHERS, DREAMWORKS, NICKELODEON, DISNEY, MARVEL FILMS, CARTOON NETWORK, HANNA BARBARA, AND TWENTIETH CENTURY FOX ON SUCH TITLES AS TRANSFORMERS: THE MOVIE, AMAZING SPIDER-MAN, TEENAGE MUTANT NINJA TURTLES, THE INCREDIBLE HULK, AND THE AVENGERS.

WRESTLING SUPER FANS
SPONSORED BY:

THE FERNANDEZ FAMILY

KARIM – THE CAPTAIN
ALEX – THE HITMAN
MISS SYLVIA
JUJU – THE CLOWN

THE FIRST FAMILY OF WRESTLING IN THE FLORIDA PANHANDLE, THE FERNANDEZ BUNCH IS A MUST-SEE ATTRACTION AT EVERY MAJOR WRESTLING AND POP CULTURE EVENT IN THE REGION.

THEY CAN BE FOUND CHIT-CHATTING WITH HALL-OF-FAMERS LIKE HACKSAW JIM DUGGAN AT CONVENTIONS, TRADING STORIES OF THE OLD DAYS IN MID-SOUTH WRESTLING. THEY BECAME FAST FRIENDS WITH ADRIAN NEVILLE – AKA PAC FROM ALL ELITE WRESTLING – AT AN NXT HOUSE SHOW AND ACTUALLY GOT ON HIS GOOD SIDE, RECEIVING WELL WISHES AND A SELFIE FROM THE INFAMOUS HEEL. AND YOU KNOW THEY DID WRESTLEMANIA XXIII TO SEE UNDERTAKER V. ROMAN REIGNS!

WRESTLING SUPER FANS

RYAN SUPPLE

OFTEN HOBNOBBING WITH THE LIKES OF DREW MCINTYRE AND JINDER MAHAL SINCE THEIR DAYS IN THE FACTION, 3MB, RYAN IS KNOWN THROUGHOUT THE INDUSTRY AS A CHAMPION-MAKER. ASPIRING BELT-HOLDERS LINED UP WHEN HE WAS SPOTTED BACKSTAGE AT WRESTLEMANIA 32, THE ROYAL RUMBLES OF 2013 AND 2020. AT THE LATTER, HE HELD COURT WITH LEGENDS OLD & NEW: TED DIBIASE, REY MYSTERIO, BECKY LYNCH & CHARLOTTE FLAIR.

DRAKE STAGE

DRAKE IS WHAT IS KNOWN IN THE BUSINESS AS AN UP-AND-COMER, WITH DESIGNS ON SPENDING MANY YEARS RINGSIDE, MANAGING EPIC-LEVEL TALENT AT THE HIGHEST TIERS OF WRESTLING. HE ALREADY HAD A SIT-DOWN WITH ONE OF THE BEST EVER, JIM CORNETTE, AND HAD THE AUDACITY TO APE CORNETTE'S STYLE WHEN HE DID IT. THAT'S THE KIND OF MOXY THAT GETS YOU A HIGH-FIVE FROM RANDY ORTON, MID-MATCH WITH JINDER MAHAL.

CAN CRUSHERS PODCAST

JOHN "THE ENGLISH PROFESSOR" & MARK "THE MARK" ARE ON THE CUTTING EDGE OF PRO WRESTLING MEDIA. THESE ROAD DOGS HAVE INTERVIEWED WRESTLEMANIA III HEROES, THE KILLER BEES. THEY'VE MINGLED WITH SUCH LUMINARIES AS THE NATURE BOY RIC FLAIR AND BIG SEXY KEVIN NASH. THEY'VE CAPTURED EVERY AUTOGRAPH OF A SLEW OF JIM CROCKETT PROMOTIONS LEGENDS AT A BIG TIME WRESTLING EVENT. THEY ARE LEGENDS!

STEVEN BRADLEY

WITH THREE FULL DECADES OF STUDYING THE SCIENCE OF WRESTLING UNDER HIS BELT, STEVEN HAS SEEN A LITTLE BIT OF IT ALL, BUT HE REMAINED A STEADFAST FAN OF THE WWF THROUGHOUT MOST OF THOSE YEARS, CRINGING AT THE DEFECTION OF HULK HOGAN BUT REVELLING IN THE EMERGENCE OF STONE COLD STEVE AUSTIN, BEFORE DISCOVERING THE INNOVATION OF THE INDIE WRESTLING SCENE AND THE USE OF VIOLENCE AS AN ARTFORM.

WRESTLING SUPER FANS

PHIL & GENIE CHALKER

PHIL & GENIE ARE NO MERE WRESTLING FANS. THEY'RE BOOKERS EXTRAORDINAIRE, BRINGING TO THEIR HOME TOWN ALL-TIME GREAT ANNOUNCER, JIM ROSS, AND EVEN BOOKING THEIR OWN PROMOTION, FANATIX WRESTLING FEDERATION, SHOWCASING THE HALL OF FAMER BULLET BOB ARMSTRONG, ALONGSIDE MATT CROSS & SERPENTICO. THEY EVEN HAD THE GALL TO SHOW UP AT A RIVAL SHOW, A TAPING OF AEW DYNAMITE IN ATLANTA.

MATTHEW PETER PHAEDONOS

MATTHEW IS A WORLD LEADER IN THE COLLECTION AND PRESERVATION OF RARE VISUAL TEXTS ON THE HISTORY OF THE WRESTLING INDUSTRY AND ITS REMARKABLE PERFORMERS. FOR YEARS, THE LAW SCHOLAR AND SPORTS ENTERTAINMENT HISTORIAN HAS BEEN AN UNFLINCHING PATRON OF SHORT-FORM BIOGRAPHIES AND CUSTOM ART DEPICTING THE MOST CRITICAL MOMENTS IN THE LIVES AND CAREERS OF THE GREATEST WRESTLERS EVER.

MICHAEL SHERAR

AS A MEDAL-WINNING RUNNER, MICHAEL IS AN ACCOMPLISHED ATHLETE IN HIS OWN RIGHT. IN COMBINATION WITH HIS PhD IN MEDICAL BIOPHYSICS, HIS TALENTS BRING A UNIQUE APPRECIATION FOR THE RARE ATHLETICISM REQUIRED FOR WRESTLERS TO SUCCEED IN THEIR HIGH-FLYING, HIGH IMPACT CAREERS. HE CERTAINLY HAS A FASCINATING PERSPECTIVE ON THE RISK OF INJURY AND THE LENGTHS TO WHICH THE SQUARED CIRCLE PUSHES A BODY.

ED GRUNYON

ED MADE HIS OWN IN-ROADS INTO THE WRESTLING INDUSTRY AND CAME OUT THE OTHER SIDE AN INSIDER IN HIS OWN RIGHT, WITH CLAIMS OF FULL KNOWLEDGE OF "WHERE THE BODIES ARE BURIED". THESE ARE BACKSTAGE SECRETS SO SENSITIVE, SO OUTRAGEOUSLY FUNNY, THAT THEY ARE BEST LEFT IN SILENCE UNTIL THEIR SUBJECTS ARE EITHER TOO DEAF OR TOO DEAD TO HEAR THEM WHEN THEY ARE ULTIMATELY REVEALED.